The Decolonial Mandela

# The Decolonial Mandela

## Peace, Justice and the Politics of Life

Sabelo J. Ndlovu-Gatsheni

berghahn
NEW YORK • OXFORD
www.berghahnbooks.com

Published in 2016 by
Berghahn Books
www.berghahnbooks.com

© 2016 Ndlovu-Gatsheni

**Library of Congress Cataloging-in-Publication Data**
Ndlovu-Gatsheni, Sabelo J., author.
The decolonial Mandela: peace, justice and the politics of life / Sabelo J.
Ndlovu-Gatsheni.
    p. cm.
Includes bibliographical references and index.
ISBN 978-1-78533-118-3 (hardback) -- ISBN 978-1-78533-296-8
(paperback) -- ISBN 978-1-78533-119-0 (ebook)
1. Mandela, Nelson, 1918-2013--Influence. 2. Anti-apartheid movements-
-South Africa--History. 3. South Africa--Politics and government. 4.
Postcolonialism--South Africa. 5. Humanism--South Africa. I. Title.
DT1974.N38 2016
968.065092--dc23

                                                        015036461

**British Library Cataloguing in Publication Data**
A catalogue record for this book is available from the British Library

ISBN 978-1-78533-118-3 hardback
ISBN 978-1-78533-296-8 paperback
ISBN 978-1-78533-119-0 ebook

*To the memory of Sentime Kasay, a humble colleague
and a dedicated young decolonial scholar, whose life was
cut short in 2013.*

*To the dedicated members of the Africa Decolonial Research
Network (ADERN). Ours is a civilizational decolonial humanist
struggle, where there is no space for bigotry, sexism, racism,
tribalism or xenophobia. Aluta Continua!*

# Contents

Preface                                                                    ix

Acknowledgements                                                          xix

Abbreviations                                                            xxii

Introduction   The Mandela Phenomenon as Decolonial
               Humanism                                                     1

One            Decolonial Theory of Life                                   35

Two            Mandela: Different Lives in One                             71

Three          Mandela at CODESA, and New
               Conceptions of Justice                                      92

Epilogue       In Search of a Paradigm of Peace                          121

References                                                               143

Index                                                                    155

# Preface

While all human species live and die, Nelson Rolihlahla Mandela will never die as a symbol of a third decolonial humanist revolution privileging the struggles of the 'anthropos of the planet' for freedom and liberation. Like all symbols of something worthwhile, unpacking and reflecting on the meanings of Mandela's life of struggle and legacy is a complex intellectual and academic undertaking. As Cornel West (2006: 13) put it, 'He constitutes such a challenge to us – an intellectual challenge, a political challenge, a moral challenge, and an existential challenge'. This is because we are trying to understand a complex political life with a global resonance and an allegory of the very birth pangs of the post-apartheid South African nation. This requires a new language of comprehension beyond the current biographical and hagiographical interventions as well as beyond the traditional liberal, Marxist and nationalist interpretations.

Indeed Mandela's life of struggle has already attracted numerous biographies and hagiographies. These biographies include F. Meer's *Higher Than Hope: Rolihlahla We Love You: Nelson Mandela's Biography on his 70th Birthday* (1988); J. Schadeberg's *Nelson Mandela and the Rise of the ANC* (1990); M. Benson's *Nelson Mandela: The Man and The Movement* (1994); M. Meredith's *Nelson Mandela: A Biography* (1997); A. Sampson's *Mandela: The Authorized Biography* (1999); T. Lodge's *Mandela: A Critical Life* (2009); Rita Barnard's *The Cambridge Companion to Nelson Mandela* (2014) and many others. His death on the 5

December 2013 provoked new writings and reflections. The collection of essays by Barnard (2014) is among the most recent critical academic reflections on various aspects of Mandela's life focusing on such important issues as antinomies of Mandela, emotions of Mandela, Mandela's relationship with modernity and tradition, Mandela and law, and Mandela and war, as well as Mandela's mortality. What is distinctive about Barnard's book is that it is a critical reflective work of various scholars on the life on Mandela but is not focused on the broader meanings of the Mandela phenomenon. The distinguished African historian Toyin Falola edited *Mandela: Tributes to a Global Icon* (2014), capturing the best eulogies on Mandela and reflecting on his virtues, greatness and contributions to the struggles for peace, justice and life itself.

But some of the earlier attempts at encapsulating the meaning of Mandela frantically tried to reduce him to a fixed ideological orientation ignoring the fact that Mandela was a symbol of a third decolonial humanist age with the capacity to embrace various ideological strands as long as they advanced the liberation struggle of the anthropos of the planet. But his life of struggle and legacy had a decolonial civilizational content for both the colonizer and the colonized. In Mandela, the erstwhile white colonizer who had fallen from humanity to the extent of enslaving and colonizing other human beings, found an invitation back into humanity. The colonized people who had been written out of the human ocumene and whose ontological density had been drained and denied had to be liberated from invented and colonially imposed inferiority complex so as to regain lost ontological density.

This book is not yet another biography of Mandela. Nor is it a eulogy of Mandela. It is a critical decolonial reflective and interpretive study of the 'Mandela phenomenon' as an idea, symbol, signifier, voice, expression, representation and resource in a political rhetoric of decolonization. The Mandela phenomenon is constitutive of a decolonial humanistic civilizational project aimed at transcending the Euro-North American-centric modernity that authorized and enabled the slave trade, imperialism, colonialism, apartheid and underdevelopment of other parts of the world. Mandela, just like other African decolonial humanists like C.L.R.

James, William E.B. Dubois, Mahatma Gandhi, Frantz Fanon, Thomas Sankara, Stephen Bantu Biko and many others, sought to decolonize, deracialize and deimperialize an asymmetrically structured world system and its imperial-colonial global orders that has been in place since the time of the onset of colonial encounters. What I call the 'Mandela phenomenon' is also a constitutive part of what Ngugi wa Thiong'o (1993) described as 'moving the centre' while remaining unrepentantly 'universalist'. Mandela is one of those African leaders whose life of struggle and legacy contributed immensely to the process of 'moving the centre' of Europe–North America-centric modernity/imperialism/colonialism/apartheid to accommodate black humanity. It entailed moving black people from the margins to the centre of the envisaged modern, genuinely decolonized and deimperialized world.

Mandela's life of struggle and legacy is an embodiment of a politics of life as defined by Enrique Dussel in his *Twenty Theses on Politics* (2008) and is a leitmotif of his *Politics of Liberation* (2011). The Mandela phenomenon is founded on decolonial politics that privileges the recognition of pluriversality as a foundation of human experience. Such a politics of life recognized the flowering of histories and cultures of different peoples of the earth as the normal state of human life that must be celebrated rather than criminalized. In this politics of life, Mandela emerges as a voice of decolonial ethical reason ranged against imperial reason. In this scheme of politics of liberation, Mandela becomes that embodiment of a paradigm of peace as opposed to the imperial paradigm of war that has been in place since the dawn of Euro-North American-centric modernity.

Elleke Boehmer (2008: 5–6) was correct in reading the Mandela phenomenon as 'a history with a nationalist moral attachment, a pedagogical tale bearing political truth'. A critical decolonial ethical analysis of the Mandela phenomenon cannot be understood as part of a simple South African micro-history. It is only fully comprehendible if pitched at the higher level of the global decolonial humanist struggles ranged against a post-Enlightenment modern world, which Ramon Grosfoguel (2007, 2011) aptly characterized as racially hierarchized, patriarchal, Euro-North

American-centric, Christian-centric, hetero-normative, capitalist, imperial and colonial. Emerging from this modernist/imperial/ colonial milieu, Mandela's life of struggle was for a broader and higher human cause – that of a new global civilization informed by a profound decolonial humanism. It is a human cause that Frantz Fanon (1968) wrote about as gesturing towards a new humanism.

In defining his place in this anti-colonial, decolonial humanist struggle, Mandela himself said: 'I am the peg on which to hang all the aspirations of the African National Congress' (quoted in Sampson 1999: 33). This book extends this self-definition of Mandela to a 'peg' on which all aspirations of those people defined by Fanon (1968) as 'the wretched of the earth' hung. Both his severe critics and those who celebrated him were pushed by the common factor of a very deep love for him. This is why some constituencies whose aspirations and expectations were not met during Mandela's life have turned out to be his worst critics because they had hung their hopes on him. What must be appreciated, however, is that the profound humanism that Mandela represented could not be realized within a span of one individual's lifetime. It is part of the ongoing global decolonization and deimperialization project that commenced at the very time of colonial encounters. It is a continuing decolonial civilizational struggle aimed at producing a new humanism that is inclusive and free from racism and coloniality.

At the centre of this unfinished project is the task of decolonizing being, the task of decolonizing knowledge, and the task of decolonizing power (Chinweizu 1975, 1987; Ake 1979; Ngugi wa Thiong'o 1986; Mignolo 1995, 2000, 2011; Quijano 2000, 2007; Grosfoguel 2007, 2011; Maldonado-Torres 2007; Ndlovu-Gatsheni 2013a, 2013b). Such decolonial and deimperial global civilizational projects should not be simplistically understood in generational or epochal terms. It is a long-term decolonial civilizational project and human struggle opposed to 'the will to power' and paradigm of war that was introduced, routinized and naturalized by Euro-North American-centric modernity and Western philosophy. Mandela represented a politics that privileged what Dussel (2008) termed 'the will to live' and the paradigm of peace.

This explains why, in this book, the Mandela phenomenon is further understood as an embodiment of a new paradigm of justice – a transitional justice that Mahmood Mamdani (2009, 2013a, 2013b) articulated as 'survivor's justice'. It is a form of transitional justice that is not based on a post-1945 Nuremberg template. Nuremberg was a victor's justice – a victor that also masqueraded as a victim. It privileged punishments of selected individuals who were identified as 'perpetrators'. A survivor's justice is premised on transformation of society emerging from mass violence to enable both 'perpetrators' and 'victims' to be reborn as new beings inhabiting a new society underpinned by a paradigm of peace. In this case, the Mandela phenomenon also encapsulated a decolonial-liberatory utopic imaginary that has remained as an unfinished business.

There is also additional interest in the persona of Mandela and its meaning. Mandela is one of those African leaders who literally walked through the shadow of death. He was tried at Rivonia for treason, which carried at that time a mandatory death sentence. Mandela also experienced an exceptionally long period of incarceration. In total, his imprisonment spanned twenty-seven years. His long life of struggle and legacy is better depicted as that of a radical African nationalist-liberal-decolonial humanist, partly because his decolonial humanism emerged in struggle and partly because his phenomenon was built on an established tradition of earlier visionary decolonial humanist leaders of the African National Congress (ANC), such as Pixley ka Isaka Seme and Chief Albert Luthuli. Mandela's principled, committed and selfless involvement in the African nationalist decolonial struggle and his legacy directly challenged the German philosopher Friedrich Nietzsche's notion of war as natural cascading from an imperial conception of politics as founded on the will to power.

Mandela as a survivor was prone to push for the paradigm of peace rather than that of war. His conception of justice was that of a survivor rather than a victor. Such a survivor's justice is superior to the victor or victim's justice that privileges criminal punishments without political transformation of society and breaking from the paradigm of war. According to Mahmood Mamdani (2009, 2013a, 2013b), survivor's justice allowed a people emerging from a situation of mass violence to move forward together, rebuilding on a new foundation and creating new identities beyond the adversarial perpetrator/victim identities of yesterday shaped by the paradigm of war.

In a conceptual sense, *The Decolonial Mandela: Peace, Justice and the Politics of Life* is a book that unpacks what it means 'to walk through the shadow of death'. Walking through the shadow of death is a colonially invented existential reality of dehumanization and death. It is constitutive of the lives of those people whom Fanon (1968) aptly described as 'the wretched of the earth', who were forced by colonialism to inhabit the 'zone of non-being'. These people were an invention of coloniality and its paradigm of war. Therefore, the act of walking through the shadow of death entailed enduring hellish conditions in a zone where suspension of ethics was the norm, and normalization of the paradigm of war was the order of life. These hellish conditions captured the essence of 'life of death' in the 'zone of non-being'. The first people to walk through the shadow of death were those Africans who were captured and sold into slavery. These African people were violently captured in the interior of Africa and transformed into slaves. Slaves lost their humanity and became commodities. They were forced to march long distances to the coast where they were bundled into the notorious slave ships. Those people sold into slavery endured the notorious 'middle passage'. They laboured in the plantations and mines. They endured various forms of brutalities as they were considered to be non-human beings. The long-term consequence of this human trafficking is symbolized by the African diaspora who have lost contact with where they originated.

The slave trade was indeed the first global heinous manifestation of the underside of modernity and its paradigm of war. The second group of people who walked through the shadow of death were the African people who were turned into colonial subjects and experienced the 'arrival of empire'. Empire arrived in Latin America, the Caribbean, Asia and Africa as a violent imperial and colonial machine. The ideologues of the empire doubted the humanity of those people they encountered outside Europe. Imperial reason underpinned and informed the activities of the empire. Imperial reason assumed the form of what Nelson Maldonado-Torres (2007) described as 'imperial Manichean misanthropic skepticism': a scepticism about the humanity of black people. Imperial reason authorized hierarchization and the profiling of people according to race.

Imperial reason informed ideas of an African continent that was empty. James Blaut (1993) distilled four core claims of notions of empty lands. The first was that areas inhabited by non-Europeans were not inhabited by any people, and were for that reason always available for European settlement. This notion of empty land fed and sustained the fallacious imperial idea of a European people who never displaced anybody from land. The second was that where people were found, they were redefined as mobile and nomadic wanderers with no claim on any territory and no sense of sovereignty. The third core aspect of the imperial idea of empty lands was that those people inhabiting lands outside Europe and North America had no idea of private property, no idea of property rights and no claims to anything including land. This notion was used to justify all forms of dispossessions, displacements and sharing of land among white settlers. The final idea was that the peoples inhabiting such spaces as Africa were bereft of intellectual creativity, lacking rationality and deficient in spiritual values (Blaut 1993; Maldonado-Torres 2004).

The consequences of imperial reason were imperialism, colonialism, apartheid, neo-colonialism and underdevelopment. These constituted coloniality as a global power structure that survived the dismantling of administrative colonialism and juridical apartheid. Within this milieu of modernity/imperial/colonial/capitalist/apartheid entanglements emerged specific notions of 'being', defined in racial terms. Being black became reproduced and represented as a form of disability, lacking something and being deficient. Such an imperial articulation of being was used to identify those who were forced to walk through the shadow of death and those who were forced to inhabit the zone of non-being. In the zone of non-being, we have mere 'inhabitants' not 'citizens' (Levander and Mignolo 2011: 3; Casimir 2011).

These are people who have been peripherized from Euro-American-centric modernity physically, intellectually and epistemologically. The same people have been perpetually and consistently engaged in a life and death struggle for humanity since the dawn of modernity. They are people who have grappled with the perennial and painful existential question of what it means to be reduced to a 'void' and 'nothingness'. In the specific case of South Africa, the apartheid colonial system physically peripherized black people by pushing them into the Bantustans, which literally existed as labour reserves and zones of non-being.

Initiatives and struggles from the Global South in general and Africa in particular have to be understood as taking a humanist format because they inevitably involve trying to emerge from a colonized being, trying to push away the big boulder of coloniality and trying to free and extricate oneself from the paradigm of war. This is why the best way to capture the life of struggle of Mandela is as an embodiment of the paradigm of peace, racial harmony, and new pluriversal humanism. This new reading of Mandela's political life and legacy is informed by a critical decolonial ethics of liberation.

The 'critical decolonial ethics of liberation' privileges paradigm of peace, humanism, and racial harmony as opposed to the imperial/colonial/apartheid paradigm of war and racial hatred. At the core of critical decolonial ethics of liberation is the unmasking of an imperial/colonial/apartheid system that was driven by the logic of racial profiling, and the classification and hierarchization of human beings. It resulted in the denial of the humanity of black people and enabled enslavement, conquest, colonization, dispossession, exploitation, and notions of impossibility of co-presence of human races. The colonization of South Africa and institutionalization of apartheid were part of broader global imperial designs and a paradigm of war. This is why the processes of insertion of South Africa into imperial/colonial modernity are contemporaneous with those of Latin America and Asia. Bartholomew Diaz circumnavigated the Cape in 1488 and Vasco da Gama reached

the East Indies in 1497 – the same period in which Christopher
Columbus reached the Americas, in 1492.

Mandela emerges at the centre of this imperial/colonial/apart-
heid milieu vehemently opposed to the paradigm of war, logic
of racism and coloniality, to the extent of being prepared to die
for the cause of democracy and human rights long before these
values were globally accepted as part of the post-Cold War international normative order. This set him apart as a decolonial ethical
humanist par excellence. Even after enduring twenty-seven years
of incarceration on the notorious Robben Island, Mandela avoided
bitterness and preached the gospel of racial harmony, reconciliation and democracy.

Mandela's leadership role during the transition from apartheid
to democracy inaugurated a shift from the Nuremberg paradigm
of justice to a new paradigm of political justice privileging political reform and social transformation as its teleology. When he
became the first black president of a democratic South Africa,
Mandela practically and symbolically made important overtures
to the erstwhile white racists, aimed at hailing them back to a new,
inclusive, non-racial, democratic and pluriversal society known as
'the rainbow nation'.

But the realities of coloniality on the ground in South Africa in
particular, and the modern world in general, have remained resistant to the project of creating another world and a new humanism.
We are living in a world that continues to create modern problems
for which it has no modern solutions. It is a world that is still dominated by multiple dimensions of social, political, cultural, sexual,
ethnic, religious, historical and ecological injustices. Boaventura
de Sousa Santos, in his recent work *Epistemologies of the South:
Justice against Epistemicide* (2014), has added cognitive injustice (that is the failure to recognize the different ways of knowing
by which people across the globe provide meaning to their existence) as another terrain of decolonial struggle in the twenty-first
century.

Mandela played his part, and his legacy left a number of lessons
for our generation to continue the global struggle for genuine
decolonization and a genuine deimperialization. Mandela is one

of those African decolonial humanists who dedicated their lives to the struggle to realize a new deimperialized pluriversal world inhabited by new people free from the scourge of race and war – a world in which a single citizenship for former colonizers and the formerly colonized is envisaged. But to realize this single citizenship embracing what Mamdani (1996) termed 'citizens' and 'subjects' would require 'an overall metamorphosis whereby erstwhile colonizers and colonized are politically reborn as equal members of a single political community' (Mamdani 1998: 10; Mamdani 2001a).

This is what Mandela fought for, 'establishing for the first time a political order based on consent and not conquest. It is about establishing a political community of equal and consenting citizens' (Mamdani 1998: 10). This decolonial humanist vision is impossible to realize under global coloniality. This is why the struggle for decolonization and deimperialization of the modern world, born in 1492 with Christopher Columbus's discovery of the 'New World', must be intensified in the twenty-first century by the current generation. The modern world system that is Euro-North American-centric is resistant to decolonization and deracialization. The global orders it has enabled are inherently colonial and imperialist, despite the rhetoric of democracy and human rights. By standing and fighting against this racist, tyrannical and imperialist modern world, Mandela became, in the words of Xolela Mangcu (2011), a 'worthy ancestor' whose life of struggle and legacy symbolized the finest traditions of the struggle for decolonial humanism.

Sabelo J. Ndlovu-Gatsheni
Pretoria, South Africa
March 2015

# Acknowledgements

It was soon after the death of Nelson Mandela on 5 December 2013 that I set out to read seriously about his life of struggle and legacy. My intention was to write what I had dubbed 'a critical decolonial tribute to Nelson Rolihlahla Mandela'. In its form and content, this was going to constitute an elongated obituary. I re-read his voluminous autobiography *Long Walk to Freedom*, this time very slowly, listening carefully to each and every message scripted therein. It was to be a retrospective reading taking place within a context in which there was an outpouring of reflective obituaries and tributes.

But no sooner had I shared the draft piece with some members of Africa Decolonial Research Network (ADERN), particularly Dr Morgan Ndlovu (Department of Development Studies, University of South Africa), Mr William Jethro Mpofu (University of South Africa), Dr Tendayi Sithole (Department of Political Sciences, University of South Africa), and Ms Akhona Nkenkana (Thabo Mbeki African Leadership Institute/Jindal Global University) than there was a distinct feeling that I should write a book that was ostensibly informed by decolonial thought and decolonial theory on Mandela's life of struggle and legacy. I would therefore like to thank these colleagues for their suggestions and support throughout the writing of this book. What we debated endlessly was the question of the role of violence in liberation struggles, and Mandela's approaches towards the resolution of the race question in South Africa. The heated debates took us back to Frantz Fanon's ideas on anti-colonial violence and its redemptive qualities, as well as the strengths and weaknesses of reconciliation. There are a number of people I would like to thank specifically. Professor Valentin Y. Mudimbe from Duke University in Durham, North Carolina, read the whole manuscript and encouraged me to complete the work for publication. Dr Siphamandla Zondi (Executive Director of Institute of Global Dialogue) not only generously forwarded alerts on new publications on Mandela ever since I told him I was writing this book but also read the whole manuscript and provided useful comments. Ms Akhona Nkenkana assisted me with drawing Figure 2.1, and I am really grateful for her kindness. My partner, Pinky Patricia Nkete, has been a strong source of support throughout the writing of this book and we debated endlessly the meaning and significance of Mandela. Professor Nelson Maldonado-Torres from Rutgers University in New Brunswick, New Jersey, whose groundbreaking work *Against War* helped me a lot to frame conceptually and theoretically my own book, was kind enough to read the first draft of an article that constituted the nucleus of this book. Ahmed Jazbay (Department of Political Sciences, University of South Africa) provided some useful written and published material on Mandela that assisted me in shaping the arguments of this book. Dr Edith Phaswana (Department of Development Studies and Anthropology, University of Johannesburg) read one of the more extended draft chapters on which this book is based, and provided useful comments. My brother, Professor Sifiso Mxolisi Ndlovu of South African Democracy Education Trust (SADET) based at the University of South Africa, carefully read the entire manuscript and not only offered me useful comments but also pointed me to further reading material that enabled me to strengthen the book. Professor Vusi Gumede, Head of Thabo Mbeki African Leadership Institute (TMALI) based at the University of South Africa, also read the entire manuscript following our heated debates over the paradigm of war versus the paradigm of peace. His critical comments were very useful.

Since the beginning of 2014, a few of us as members of ADERN have been meeting informally on Fridays after work in a small 'corner' of the Burgers Park Hotel's Diplomat Bar to reflect on many contemporary issues from a critical decolonial perspective. What preoccupied us most were the ideas of paradigm of war versus paradigm of peace, as well as notions of political justice versus criminal justice. In that 'corner', we have shared ideas with Professor Ramon Grosfoguel (University of California, Berkeley), Professor Boaventura de Sousa Santos (University of Coimbra, Portugal) and Professor Mammo Muchie (Tshwane University of Technology, South Africa). These informal meetings, over glasses of beer and wine, have been very helpful in exploring the applicability of decolonial thought and decolonial theory to various contemporary challenges and problems. I therefore thank most sincerely the 'regulars' to this corner, not only for their commitment to the agenda of decoloniality but also for their challenging and incisive comments, which always made me think more critically about some of the issues contained in this book. Professor Kgomotso Masemola (Department of English Studies, University of South Africa) assisted with some editorial interventions that improved the readability of this book. Finally, I thank the three anonymous reviewers for providing critical comments that enabled me to consolidate the manuscript into its present published form. I, however, take full responsibility for all the arguments raised in this book, as well as for any errors.

# Abbreviations

| | |
|---|---|
| ADERN | Africa Decolonial Research Network |
| AIM | Academic-Institutional-Media |
| ANC | African National Congress |
| ANCYL | African National Congress Youth League |
| APLA | Azania People's Liberation Army |
| AZAPO | Azania People's Organization |
| BCM | Black Consciousness Movement |
| CDE | Critical Decolonial Ethics |
| CODESA | Convention for a Democratic South Africa |
| COPE | Congress of the People |
| COSATU | Congress of South African Trade Unions |
| CP | Conservative Party |
| DA | Democratic Alliance |
| DBSA | Development Bank of Southern Africa |
| EFF | Economic Freedom Fighters |
| EPG | Eminent Persons Group |
| ETG | Economic Trends Group |

| | |
|---|---|
| GEAR | Growth, Employment and Redistribution |
| ICC | International Criminal Court |
| IDRC | International Development Research Centre |
| IFP | Inkatha Freedom Party |
| IMF | International Monetary Fund |
| MEC | Mineral Energy Complex |
| MERG | Macro-Economic Research Group |
| MK | Mkonto we Sizwe |
| MPNF | Multiparty Negotiating Forum |
| NEC | National Executive Committee |
| NEM | Normative Economic Model |
| NP | National Party |
| PAC | Pan-Africanist Congress |
| PAFMESCA | Pan-African Freedom Movement for East, Central and Southern Africa |
| RDP | Reconstruction and Development Programme |
| SABC | South Africa Broadcasting Corporation |
| SACP | South African Communist Party |
| SADF | South African Defence Forces |
| SADET | South African Democracy Trust |
| SAP | South Africa Police |
| SAPs | Structural Adjustment Programmes |
| TRC | Truth and Reconciliation Commission |
| UN | United Nations |

# Introduction

# The Mandela Phenomenon as Decolonial Humanism

> We must not let the men who worship war and who lust after blood, precipitate actions that will plunge our country into another Angola
> – Nelson Mandela, *Conversations With Myself*

> If one wanted an example of an unshakably firm, courageous, heroic, calm, intelligent, and capable man, that example and that man would be Mandela. ...
> I identify him as one of the most extraordinary symbols of this era.
> – Fidel Castro, in Waters, *Nelson Mandela and Fidel Castro*

> Let us not make Nelson Mandela some kind of icon on a pedestal belonging to a museum. He is a wave in an ocean, part of a rich tradition that raises certain kinds of questions, beginning with our own lives and our willingness to muster the courage to examine who we are as humans.
> – Cornel West, 'Nelson Mandela'

> We have to pass through the shadow of death again and again before we reach the mountain tops of our desires.
> – Nelson Mandela, in Joffe, The *State vs. Nelson Mandela*

To be a realist utopian in our time is to go beyond the present reality of the non-ethical paradigm of war as the central leitmotif of coloniality. It is to embrace decolonial theory of life; to articulate and advocate for survivor's justice aimed at radical political

1

transformation of society emerging from mass violence and that is opposed to traditional Nuremberg and International Criminal Court paradigm of criminal justice; and to demonstrate deep commitment to the paradigm of peace as opposed to the paradigm of war. Nelson Rolihlahla Mandela not only epitomized survivor's justice but became a metaphor for new pluriversal humanism, peace, reconciliation and racial harmony.

Located at the interface of complex national, continental and global vortex of modern politics, the Mandela phenomenon that is subjected to analysis in this book is an authentically African invention and achievement that emerged and crystallized in the course of the anti-imperial, anti-colonial, anti-apartheid and anti-global coloniality struggles. Like all other embodiments of positive values, the Mandela phenomenon became open to theft. The distinguished social anthropologist Jack Goody's book *The Theft of History* (2006) is very instructive and prompts us to be on our guard against theft of all positive aspects of human history by advocates of Eurocentrism and the Athens-to-Washington paradigm. The Athens-to-Washington paradigm was coined by the leading African historian Paul Tiyambe Zeleza (2007) to capture the Eurocentric idea of rendering human civilization as originating in Greece and reaching its mature stage in present day United States of America. This rendition of human history is a form of usurpation/theft of world history and the story of human civilizations. In South Africa, attempts at stealing the Mandela phenomenon have been underway since he was released from prison. The theft is spearheaded by those who even supported the incarceration of Mandela and his criminalization as a 'dangerous terrorist' during the heydays of apartheid. The very fact that Mandela had to receive the Nobel Peace Prize concurrently with FW de Klerk (the last apartheid president) on 10 December 1993 was the beginning of attempts at stealing the Mandela phenomenon by his adversaries. The harnessing of Mandela's name with that of leading imperialist Cecil John Rhodes to create the Mandela Rhodes Foundation is another glaring attempt at stealing the thunder from an African advocate of pluriversal decolonial humanism who was opposed to imperialism, colonialism and apartheid (Adebajo 2010).

The Nigerian scholar Adekeye Adebajo described conjoining the names of Mandela and Rhodes as 'a monstrous marriage', even though Mandela himself saw it as an initiative signalling 'the closing of the circle and the coming together of two strands in our history' (Adebajo 2010: 215). As put by Adebajo (ibid.: 217), was this not part of the attempts at rehabilitation of 'a grotesque imperialist of the nineteenth century' through associating it with the name of a leading black anti-imperialist decolonial freedom fighter of the twentieth century? This question was also posed by the historian Paul Maylam in his book *The Cult of Rhodes* (2005: 134): 'The arch-imperialist colonizer of the nineteenth century was being conjoined with the great anti-imperialist freedom fighter of the twentieth century'. Adebajo (2010: 232) posed a penetrating question: 'Has Mandela perhaps taken reconciliation too far, in rehabilitating an evil figure that Africans really should condemn to the pit-latrine of history?' Money (10 million pounds) was used by the Rhodes Trust in Oxford to ensure that the name of an imperialist Cecil John Rhodes was conjoined with that of the African decolonial humanist Nelson Mandela. This conjoining becomes even more detestable in the context of the ongoing student-led Rhodes Must Fall Movement. This movement commenced in 2015 as a call by the students at University of Cape Town in South Africa for the removal of Rhodes' statue. Rhodes' statue is one of the many relics of South Africa's colonial and apartheid imperial and colonial past that are considered offensive by the current generation of black South Africans. While the statue of Rhodes has been removed, the Rhodes Must Fall Movement has developed into a new decolonial struggle for decolonization of South African landscape through removal of colonial statues, change of colonial names, transformation of universities, and curriculum change.

One of the political parties of South Africa, the right-wing neo-liberal Democratic Alliance (DA) led by Helen Zille, is also using Mandela's name in its pursuit of neo-liberal politics and policies that are a far cry from the noble agenda of decolonization and deimperialization of the world that Mandela stood for. This appropriation/theft of Mandela is part of the broader and long-standing Euro-North American-centric modernity's modus operandi

3

of colonizing space (discovery and cartography), time (cutting it into pre-modern and modern), being (racial classification and hierarchization of human species) and nature (its reduction into a natural resource) in its drive towards usurpation of human history. At the centre of this usurpation are numerous claims 'to having invented a range of value-laden institutions such as "democracy", mercantile "capitalism", freedom, individualism' (Goody 2006: 1). With specific regard to Mandela, even once the white-dominated Communist Party of South Africa (CPSA) – now the South African Communist Party (SACP) – had even frantically tried to confiscate Mandela to the extent that Joe Slovo, a leading South African communist, claimed that they sent Mandela to the African continent in the 1960s as a communist and he came back as a nationalist (Ellis 2011).

This book is at once a defence of the decolonial Mandela as well as a critical articulation of the Mandela phenomenon as an African invention with a global reach. The study is consistently on guard against the theft of what Mandela's life of struggle and legacy stood for by advocates of Eurocentrism and liberals who loudly proclaim ideals of democracy and human rights without commitment to genuine decolonization of the modern Euro-North American-centric world system and deimperialization of the present asymmetrical global order. At the centre of the Mandela phenomenon is an admixture of decolonial humanism and undying Thembu aristocratic-monarchical cultural background, which are both vehemently opposed to domination, imperialism, colonialism and apartheid. This is typical of most African people who were born during the fading moments of African history and culture and into the emerging colonial modernity. This made him to be a man of two worlds. Mandela is very explicit on this:

> Western civilization has not entirely rubbed off my African background and I have not forgotten the days of my childhood when we used to gather round community elders to listen to their wealth of wisdom and experience. That was the custom of our forefathers and the traditional school in which we were brought up. I respect our elders and like to chat to them about olden times and when we had our own government and lived freely. (Mandela 2010: 22)

Colonialism could not easily erase African history and culture. The rural African society of Eastern Cape, within which Mandela was born, still retained its strong African identity, culture and values. Ubuntu (humanness) permeated African society, in the process engendering particular forms of governance, democracy and human rights. Governance was not clouded in complex institutional arrangements. African chiefs practised governance directly in their courts, and Mandela was a close observer of this at the court of Chief Jongintaba Dalindyebo. This is why his decolonial humanism became about the will to live for those people who have been reduced to the status of the anthropos of the planet and who had been forced to abandon their history, culture and values. In a way, the whole of Nelson Rolihlahla Mandela's life and legacy is nothing but an encapsulation of a legendary and epic discourse of African decolonial struggle in general and the embodiment of the political trajectory of South Africa from colonialism, through apartheid, through liberation struggle, to democracy and rainbow nation, in particular. Mandela expressed his humanist orientation when he said:

> The anchor of all my dreams is the collective wisdom of mankind as a whole. I am influenced more than ever before by the conviction that social equality is the only basis of human happiness ... It is around these issues that my thoughts revolve. They are centred on humans, the ideas for which they strive; on the new world that is emerging; the new generation that declares total war against all forms of cruelty, against any social order that upholds economic privilege for a minority and that condemns the mass of the population to poverty and disease, illiteracy and the host of evils that accompany a stratified society. (Mandela 2010: 183)

At the centre of the Mandela phenomenon, is the painful reality of a black people, including Mandela himself, who had to walk through the shadow of death as part of struggling for life itself in a racist/imperial/colonial/apartheid environment that demeaned and denied black people life chances. The racist/imperial/colonial/apartheid thinking that dominated South Africa between 1652 and 1994 enabled the colonial/apartheid ideologues to toy with two resolutions to what became known as the nigger/native question:

genocide or reduction of blacks to providers of cheap labour (hewers of wood and drawers of water). But even after the imperative of colonial/apartheid primitive accumulation had dictated that black people were useful as sources of cheap labour, colonialists continued to expose them to various forms of brutalities and exploitation, making their lives to be easily dispensable. This is a theme that is well analysed by the leading South African sociologist and historian Bernard Makhosezwe Magubane in his *Race and the Construction of the Dispensable Other* (2007). Being a dispensable 'Other' is part of being forced to walk through the shadow of death. Using a rich array of primary sources, Magubane examined the way in which black people came to be enslaved, denigrated, likened to animals, and regarded as the inferior, dispensable 'Other.' This process was foundational to the proliferation of racism.

This present book is not another 'glossy coffee-table' celebratory biography of Mandela. It is a deep, critical decolonial ethical reflection on an epic decolonial struggle in which Mandela played an important symbolic and substantive role. The book situates this struggle and Mandela's role within a wider canvas of the post-1492 modern, racially hierarchized world system and its colonial global orders that enabled and authorized not only a paradigm of war but also the slave trade, imperialism and colonialism. It is about Mandela as a symbol and substance of a third humanist civilizational revolution and an embodiment of an important utopic vision of a post-racial world.

The book is not necessarily about Mandela the person, but about Mandela the idea, the symbol, the historian of decolonial humanism and theoretician of freedom. Mandela as a historian of decolonial humanism had this clear conception of the genealogies and trajectories of the South African decolonial humanist struggle:

> We are the heirs to a three-stream heritage; an inheritance that inspires us to fight and die for the loftiest ideals in life. The title 'African hero' embraces all these veterans. Years later, more articulate and sophisticated personalities were to follow and, in the process, the tableau of history was enriched a thousand times – the Selope Themas, Jabavus, Dubes, Abdurahmans, Gools, Asvats,

Cachalias, and now you and your generation have joined this legion of honour. (Mandela 2010: 17)

The first stream in Mandela's rendition of decolonial humanist struggle is traceable to the San and the Khoi Khoi, whose legendary leader Autshumayo became the first South African black prisoner to be incarcerated on Robben Island. One of the leaders of the Khoi Khoi, called Klaas Stuurman, articulated a profoundly nationalist demand when he said:

> Restore the country which our fathers were despoiled by the Dutch and we have nothing more to ask. We have lived very contentedly before these Dutch plunderers molested us, and why should we not do so again if left to ourselves? Has not Groot Baas given plenty [of] grass roots, and barriers and grasshoppers for our use; and, till the Dutch destroyed them, [an] abundance of wild animals to hunt? And will they not return and multiply when these destroyers are gone? (Quoted in Newton-King 1981: 17)

History give testimony to the fact that indeed the Khoisan bore the brunt of the first colonial efforts by 'white settlers to implement the logic of a herrenvolk state in which "people of colour, however numerous and acculturated they may be, are treated as permanent aliens or outsiders"' (Halisi 1999: 28). Following this logic, Mandela was correct to notice that: 'These are the men who strove for a free South Africa long before we reached the field. They blazed the trail and it is their joint efforts that supply the source of the vast stream of SA history' (Mandela 2010: 16–17). What is emerging from this rendition of African resistance is a Mandela who was a nationalist-decolonial humanist historian. African nationalist historiography is well known for having inaugurated a new articulation of African history in terms of 'domination' and 'resistance'. Africanist historians also played an active role in demonstrating an indelible link between primary resistance and modern nationalist struggles.

But this book is not only about Mandela as a historian of the African decolonial humanist struggle, it is also about him as an embodiment of a paradigm of peace and an advocate of post-racial pluriversal humanism. It is a timely book that is written at a time dominated by global phenomenology of uncertainty and scarcity of ethical and principled leadership. It is a world locked in a paradigm of war, a world bereft of humanness, goodness, love, peace, humility, forgiveness, trust and optimism. Viewed from this vantage point, Mandela becomes at once a fighter for freedom as well as a symbol of hope for a better future that is free of racism. His life of struggle was indeed inextricably interwoven with the broader long walk of African people to freedom that is constitutive of the third decolonial humanist revolution.

The book is therefore meant to be a refreshing critical reflective work on the role (both symbolic and substantive) of an African leader who played an important part in an epic decolonial struggle, in the process enabling his people to enter a new journey of 'freedom to be free' that took a new form in 1994; it is also a deep reading *into* the recesses of Mandela rather than a simple reading *from* Mandela's real life. In this way the book opens a broader canvas on the meanings of Mandela, placing them within a world that since 1492 has remained racially hierarchized, patriarchal, sexist, imperial, colonial and capitalist (Mignolo 2000; Grosfoguel 2007; Ndlovu-Gatsheni 2013b, 2013c). This approach enables this book to delve deeper into foundational political and humanist questions of being, power and knowledge, while at the same time challenging the Nietzschean conception of politics as constituted by the will to power. It poses Mandela's life of struggle and legacy as an embodiment of the will to live of a people that Frantz Fanon termed the 'wretched of the earth'. To Mandela, politics was a vocation rather than a profession, hence he escaped the traps of 'fetishism of power' (Dussel 2008).

## Organization and Scope

The book is organized into five sections. The first section is this prologue, which delineates the parameters of the book, expresses its conceptual orientation, and introduces Mandela as a central subject of the study and a representative of the third humanist revolution. It outlines the various springs from which Mandela drew ideological power while at the same time highlighting some contestations over the meaning and legacy of Mandela.

The first chapter provides a theoretical framework in which such concepts as decoloniality, critical decolonial ethics of liberation, paradigm of war, paradigm of peace, and pluriversalism are defined and evaluated in terms of their conceptual value in understanding the Mandela phenomenon. It locates Mandela historically and discursively in the broader modern world in which forces of Hellenocentrism, Westernization and Eurocentrism emerged and shaped the world in the image of Europe and North America. At the centre of these inimical processes were imperial reason and racism that enabled imperialism, colonialism, apartheid and underdevelopment. Mandela's people – the African people – were pushed by these processes to inhabit the zone of non-being, governed according to the dictates of the paradigm of war. Mandela emerges in this chapter as a freedom fighter and decolonial humanist who creatively engaged with various ideologies in the process synthesizing these into liberatory resources. It is in this chapter that Mandela is portrayed grappling with the pertinent question of use of violence in the advancement of a decolonial humanist struggle that was itself opposed to violence, as well as with the global idea of freedom.

While this book is not biographical, but it would be incomplete without delving deeper into Mandela's various lives and different faces. Therefore, Chapter 2 is at once focused on the highlights of Mandela's life while elaborating on his political formation and consciousness development, revealing the inevitable antinomies, contradictions and ambivalences cascading from the exigencies of the liberation struggle. This chapter provides a context within which the global iconoclastic figure of Mandela crystallized.

The third chapter is a critical evaluation of Mandela's leadership during the negotiations, in the process highlighting the complexities and challenges that faced the liberation movements, the pressures that the African National Congress (ANC) and Mandela in particular were subjected to by the corporate sector that sought to maintain the economic status quo, and their international allies who were pushing for globalization of the Washington Consensus and its neo-liberal dispensation. Of central importance in this chapter is a decolonial analysis of the

Convention for a Democratic South Africa (CODESA) negotiations as signalling a departure from the Nuremberg paradigm, which privileges the victor and victim's justice whose teleology is criminal prosecution and punishments of individuals to a broader and new paradigm of political justice issuing from a survivor's desk, and privileging political reform and overall metamorphosis of settler/native/perpetrator/victim identities (Mamdani 2013a, 2013b). This chapter ends with an analysis of the character of the Mandela presidency (1994–98), with a particular focus on nation-building and economic policies.

The last section is an epilogue that further fleshes out the idea of why it is necessary in the twenty-first century for Africans in particular, and those people from the Global South in general, to continue the struggle for a post-racial pluriversal world. The epilogue identifies the key issues that make the search for a paradigm of peace difficult to realize: egocentrism that breeds and enables the conflictual politics of alterity; the myth of a world without others; the colour line; and the perennial problem of 'blackism' on a world scale. It ends with a return to Mandela's search for a peaceful world, and his active role in conflict resolution on the African continent.

Methodologically, the book is predicated on a new and refreshing decolonial reading of the idea and place of Mandela in global history and humanist revolutions (Renaissance humanism, Enlightenment humanism, and the current decolonial humanism) that is opening up the 'biography' in his autobiography (*Long Walk to Freedom*) to a broader interpretation from the vantage point of experiences emanating from what Walter Mignolo (2000) termed 'colonial difference' and Nelson Maldonado-Torres (2008a: 240) termed 'altericity' ('a distinct conception of peace, of interhuman contact and of the very meaning of the human', encapsulating 'the gift' of self-representation and 'entry' of those who have been written out of human history back into history and humanity). The autobiography is reinterpreted decolonially as a testimonial script of the political figure of Mandela as a signifier of critical decolonial ethics of liberation and articulator of a paradigm of peace and racial harmony in a world and society where a paradigm of war and racial hatred has been institutionalized since the time of colonial encounters in the fifteenth century.

However, this decolonial approach and intervention is not in any way blind to the limits of autobiographies, which are by definition carefully edited, choreographed, retrospective and expedient personal accounts that place the political self at the centre of a given historical period and cast that life in a distinctly positive and heroic light. Mandela himself explained why he presented the story of his life the way he did, and in the process revealed the logic and sensitivities that had to be taken into account:

The story of one's life should deal frankly with political colleagues, their personalities and their views. The reader would like to know what kind of a person the writer is, his relationships with others, and these should emerge not from the epithets used but from the facts themselves. *But an autobiography of a freedom fighter must inevitably be influenced by the question [of] whether the revelation of certain facts, however true they may be, will help advance the struggle or not. If the disclosure of such facts will enable us to see problems clearly and bring nearer our goal then it is our duty to do so, however much such revelations may adversely affect the particular individuals concerned. But frankness which creates unnecessary tensions and divisions which may be exploited by the enemy and retard the struggle as a whole is dangerous and must be avoided.* The utmost caution becomes particularly necessary where an autobiography is written clandestinely in prison, where one deals with political colleagues who themselves live under the hardships and tensions of prison life, who are in daily contact with officials who have a mania for persecuting prisoners. *Writing under such conditions the temptation is strong to mention only those things which will make your fellow prisoners feel that their sacrifices have not been in vain, that takes their mind away from the grim conditions in which they live and that makes them happy and hopeful.* An essential part of that caution and fair play would be to have the widest possible measure of consultation with your colleagues about what you intend to say about them, to circulate your manuscript and give them the opportunity of stating their views on any controversial issue discussed so that the facts themselves may accurately reflect the standpoints of all concerned, whatever may be the comments of the writer on those facts. Unfortunately the conditions in which I [wrote] this story, especially security considerations, made it impossible to consult any but a handful of my friends. (Mandela 2010: 209–10; my emphasis)

Mandela's explanation of how he wrote his autobiography and the sensitivities he had to navigate is very important for all those using *Long Walk to Freedom: The Autobiography of Nelson Mandela* as a primary source of information. It is partly an autobiography and partly about other freedom fighters and the trajectories of the decolonial struggle itself. Even the ambiguities and contradictions (antinomies) that Mandela struggled to transcend, which are highlighted in this book in an endeavour to avoid a simplistic celebratory approach, are partly those of the struggle itself. My book therefore provides a broader canvas on which the paradigm of war and paradigm of peace are not in any way reduced to a single event (the South African transition from apartheid to democracy), and a biography in which an exceptional singular personality (Mandela in this case) played a singular part without the assistance of other freedom fighters. What is under interpretation is the Mandela phenomenon as a broader discursive decolonial civilizational project opposed to the Euro-North American-centric civilization project that commenced in 1492.

The central subject of this book is the meaning(s) of Mandela, what he stood for, and what he symbolized in a world that decolonial theorists have described as racially hierarchized, patriarchal, hetero-normative, imperial, colonial, capitalist, Christian-centric, Euro-North-American-centric, and modern (Quijano 2000, 2007; Grosfoguel 2007, 2011; Mignolo 2011). Mandela not only experienced racial discrimination but also a long period of incarceration, and he even walked through the shadow of death. Like other humanists from the Global South such as Aime Cesaire, William E.B. Dubois, Frantz Fanon and many others, Mandela experienced and endured the consequences of being a racialized and dehumanized subject as well as being written out of the human ocumene and being reduced to dispensability. Uniquely and paradigmatically, instead of this experience turning Mandela into a monster in the Nietzschean sense, he emerged from it fighting for a new world governed and informed by a paradigm of peace and underpinned by principles of pluriversal humanism and co-humanness.

The 'Mandela phenomenon' is subject to many interpretations. This book offers a critical decolonial ethical interpretation that rearticulates the 'Mandela phenomenon' as an embodiment of a new paradigm of peace and justice in South Africa in which the erstwhile disputants lived together as born again new citizens, collectively agreeing that apartheid was an evil colonial system and vowing to work together to create a rainbow nation. However, the book acknowledges that dismantling racism and creating a postracial pluriversal society remain as Mandela's major 'unfinished projects' simply because the modern world system is resistant to decolonization and the global orders are impervious to deimperialization. It needs a decolonial civilizational project, of which Mandela was a committed foot soldier until the end of his life on 5 December 2013.

## Mandela as Symbol of the Third Humanist Revolution

The third decolonial humanist revolution is a long-standing liberation struggle, albeit still incomplete. The historical genesis of this decolonial humanist revolution can be traced to the antislave revolts. Those who approach it from the diaspora perspective highlight the Haitian Revolution of 1804 as its beginning. But within the African continent, African struggles against various forms of colonialism have a longer genealogy. But what is clear is that genealogically speaking the third humanist revolution must be traceable to all the struggles of all those people who were excluded from the Renaissance and Enlightenment Eurocentric conceptions of the human. The decolonial philosopher Nelson Maldonado-Torres (2008a: 115) articulated this decolonial humanist revolution as 'a third humanist revolution that has existed alongside the Renaissance and the Enlightenment, always pointing to their constitutive exclusions and aiming to provide a more consistent narrative of the affirmation of the value of the entire human species'.

At the centre of this revolution has been the question of the ontology of those excluded human beings from the existing conceptions of the human. Such initiatives and ideological/intellectual/political creations as Garveyism, Ethiopianism, Negritude, African Personality, Concienscism, Pan-Africanism, African

Socialism, and Black Consciousness Movement (BCM), right up to the revived African Renaissance, were produced within the context and course of African decolonial humanist struggle. Garveyism and Pan-Africanism emerged in the diaspora and spoke to the fundamental problems of blackism on a world scale. Garveyism particularly claimed 'Africa for Africans' and envisioned a return home of those African people who had been exported as slaves. Pan-Africanism emphasized the solidarity and unity of black races across the world. At the continental level, it spoke to the crucial aspect of unity of all black people.

Negritude was a specific response to the limits of the French colonial policy of assimilation that claimed to assimilate black people into French culture as a certificate to enjoy French citizenship and rights. Practically, French racism made some of the assimilated black people try to reclaim their Africanness (their negritude) as part of fighting against colonial racism and domination. The same was true of African Personality; it was a rehabilitative initiative aimed at dealing with various forms of alienation and 'name-lessness' within the context of colonial racism. The 'black consciousness' strand of African decolonial thought aimed at reversing the imposed condition of black racial inferiority as an essential prerequisite of liberation. African socialism was directly provoked by the reality of capitalist exploitation that enabled exploitation of human beings by other human beings.

But broadly speaking, in the decolonial theory of the human, the first humanist revolution was during the Renaissance, when a 'shift from a God-centred worldview to a Man-centred conception of selves, others, and world' was initiated (Maldonado-Torres 2008a: 106). The second was the Enlightenment humanism, which Immanuel Kant (1996: 58) celebrated as mankind's emergence and liberation from 'self-incurred immaturity' resulting in the creation of modern institutions ranging from Inquisition, the nation-state, modern racial slavery, to the establishment of universities as centres of studying the humanities (see also Maldonado-Torres 2008a: 109).

What is distinctive about the third humanist revolution is that it is driven by thinkers, activists and intellectuals from the Global

South who have experienced the undersides of modernity including enslavement and colonization. Global South thinkers motivate for a new humanist-oriented modernity that is inevitably predicated on decolonizing and deimperializing the world as part of breaking from the paradigm of war. Its horizon is the regaining of ontological density by black people and the creation of a new and inclusive post-racial pluriversality. Unless racism is transcended successfully and in good faith, the third humanist revolution cannot be realized.

But two of the major obstacles to human liberation and flourishing identified in this book are the paradigm of war and racism. It was the German philosopher Friedrich Nietzsche in *The Will to Power* (1968) who articulated the core contours of the paradigm of war, insisting that war was the natural state of things and that human beings were destined to rarely want peace – and if they did so it was for brief periods of time. To Nietzsche (ibid.: 550) 'the world is the will to power', dominated by human beings who were always attempting to impose their will on others. According to Nietzsche, there were no truly altruistic human actions and the idea of selfless action was discounted as a psychological error informed by Judeo-Christian thought.

According to Nietzsche (1968: 382), 'the commandment to love one's neighbor has never yet been extended to include one's actual neighbor'. It was the same Nietzsche (1909 [1990: 102]) who posited: 'He who fights with monsters should look to it that he himself does not become a monster ... When you gaze long into an abyss the abyss gazes into you'. Here Nietzsche was addressing the other important aspect of the paradigm of war – that of dehumanizing its victims and making them see war as natural, in the process falling into what Frantz Fanon (1968) understood as 'repetition without change'. In this case, the 'repetition without change' takes the form of embracing the paradigm war and degenerating into what Jean-Paul Sartre termed 'anti-racist racism' in one's search and struggle for peace and new humanism. The post-1945 decolonization project has not yet delivered an Africa that is free from the paradigm of war. In many places, racism has mutated

**15**

and assumed different markers including tribalism, regionalism and xenophobia.

Mandela's life of struggle and legacy challenges the paradigm of war and its ability to turn those who were involved in the liberation struggle against such monstrosities as imperialism, colonialism, apartheid, neocolonialism and coloniality into becoming monsters themselves. Deployment of critical decolonial ethics of liberation is meant to open a canvas on the meaning of Mandela and to articulate that he stood for a paradigm of peace. Mandela's life of struggle became an embodiment of pluriversal humanism (a world in which many worlds fit) (see Mignolo 2011). A pluriversal world is opposed to the paradigm of war and racial hatred that emerged at the dawn of a Euro-North American-centric modernity. The paradigm of war is founded on the politics of racial hatred and denial of humanity of black people, which is part of the darker side/underside of modernity (see Mignolo 1995, 2000, 2011).

Apartheid colonialism and the apartheid regime that came to power in South Africa in 1948 were a typical manifestation of this darker side/underside of modernity. It had survived the early decolonization processes of the 1960s and it continued to defy global anti-apartheid onslaught until 1994. Apartheid existed as a form of coloniality, which is not only a darker side/underside of modernity which has survived direct administrative colonialism but is also a constitutive element of the paradigm of war (Maldonado-Torres 2007; Ndlovu-Gatsheni 2013a, 2013b). Anibal Quijano (2000, 2007), a leading Peruvian sociologist, defined coloniality as a global power structure underpinned by four invisible colonial matrices of power, namely *control of the economy* based on appropriation of natural resources including land and labour as well as finance of indebted countries; *control of authority* through imperial institutions and use of military and sophisticated technology; *control of gender and sexuality* through projection of Christian, bourgeois and monogamous family as a model for the rest of the world and naturalization of human heterosexual relations; *control of knowledge and subjectivity* through universalization of rationalist-scientific Euro-North American-centric epistemology drawing from the Cartesian *cogito* (see Grosfoguel 2007; Maldonado-Torres 2007).

While situating Mandela within the broader decolonial canvas, the book also highlights the complexities of the Mandela phenomenon as that which is open to different interpretation. The critical decolonial ethical interpretation is just one of them. Fidel Castro's reflections on the life of struggle and legacy of Mandela emphasized the symbolic aspect: 'one of the most extraordinary symbols of this era' (Castro in Waters 1991: 31). This is why in this book Mandela is approached as at once a historian of the South African struggle for decolonial liberation and a theoretician of decolonial freedom who demonstrated a deep understanding of the meaning and essence of freedom. This is evident from his celebrated autobiography in which he reflected deeply on the trajectory of freedom and the meaning of what was achieved in 1994 in these profound words:

> The truth is that we are not yet free; we merely achieved the freedom to be free, the right not to be oppressed. We have not taken the final step of our journey, but the first step on a longer and even more difficult road. For, to be free is not merely to cast off one's chains, but to live in a way that respects and enhances the freedom of others. The task of our devotion to freedom is just beginning. (Mandela 1994: 544)

## But Who and What Influenced Mandela?

The Mandela phenomenon is watered from many springs. It was at the end of the traditional initiation ceremony involving circumcision that Mandela not only received a new name, 'Dalibhunga' – meaning 'Founder of the Bungha, the traditional body of Transkei/maker of parliaments' – but was also introduced to his first profound decolonial lesson from Chief Meligqili, son of Dalindyebo, in his delivery of the expected congratulatory homily to the new initiates. While the initiates were excited about their entry into manhood, Chief Meligqili told them that the ritual's promise to be a real entry into manhood was empty, illusory and hollow. He explained to the initiates:

There sit our sons, young, healthy and handsome, the flower of the Xhosa tribe, the pride of our nation. We have just circumcised them in a ritual that promises them manhood, but I am here to tell you that it is an empty, illusory promise, a promise that can never be fulfilled. For we Xhosas, and all black South Africans, are a conquered people. We are slaves in our own country. We are tenants on our own soil. We have no strength, no power, no control over our own destiny in the land of our birth. They will go to the cities where they will live in shacks and drink cheap alcohol, all because we have no land to give them where they could prosper and multiply. They will cough their lungs out deep in the bowels of the white man's mines destroying their health, so that the white man can live a life of unequalled prosperity. Among these young men are chiefs who will never rule because we have no power to govern ourselves; soldiers who will never fight for we have no weapons to fight with; scholars who will never teach because we have no place for them to study. The abilities, the intelligence, the promise of these young men will be squandered in their attempt to eke out a living doing the simplest, most mindless chores for the white man. These gifts today are naught, for we cannot give them the greatest gift of all, which is freedom and independence. I well know that Qamata [God] is all-seeing and never sleeps, but I have a suspicion that Qamata may in fact be dozing. If this is the case, the sooner I die the better, because then I can meet him and shake him awake and tell him that the children of Ngubencuka, the flower of the Xhosa nation, are dying. (Quoted in Mandela 1994: 27–28)

Chief Meligqili opened the eyes of the initiates to realize that they were not entering manhood as free people. They were in fact entering a dehumanizing colonial/apartheid world in which black people were considered perpetual children. The second decolonial teacher that Mandela met as a young boy was the great Xhosa poet/praise singer (*imbongi*) and oral historian Krune Mqhayi. Despite the fact that the Xhosa and all black indigenous people were now a defeated and colonized people, Mqhayi still exuded a pre-colonial Africa in his attire. He wore leopard-skin kaross and carried a spear.

Mqhayi, just like Chief Meligqili, reminded the students of the significance of the spear: 'The assegai stands for what is glorious and true in African history; it is a symbol of the African as warrior and the African as artist' (quoted in Mandela 1994: 39). During his performance, his spear had accidentally hit the modern curtain wire above him and he took advantage of this incident to deliver a decolonial lesson to the students, explaining that the striking of the curtain wire by the spear symbolized the clash between African culture and that of Europe. He elaborated:

> What I am talking about is not a piece of bone touching a piece of metal, or even the overlapping of one culture and another; what I am talking about is the brutal clash between what is indigenous and good, and what is foreign and bad. We cannot allow these foreigners who do not care for our culture to take over our nation. I predict that, one day, the forces of African society will achieve a momentous victory over the interloper. For too long we have succumbed to the false gods of the white man. But we shall emerge and cast off these foreign notions. (Quoted in Mandela 1994: 39)

Mandela expressed how he was galvanized and conscientized politically by Mqhayi to challenge white supremacy. When he reached Johannesburg he was politicized by Gaur Radebe who was not simply a clerk, interpreter and messenger in a white-owned legal firm but a political activist and effective mobilizer of black people against colonial injustices who told his white employers: 'You people stole our land from us and enslaved us. Now you are making us pay through the nose to get the worst pieces of it back' (Quoted in Mandela 1994: 68). It was Radebe that influenced Mandela to participate in the bus boycott in 1942. On how he was influenced by Radebe, Mandela wrote:

> But what Gaur Radebe knew was far more than I did because he learned not only just facts; he was able to get behind the facts and explain to you the causes for a particular viewpoint. And I learnt history afresh and I met a number of them. (Mandela 2010: 43)

Radebe was one of the early South African organic intellectuals. His academic background was very humble but he had profound knowledge about the black condition in South Africa. In Johannesburg, Mandela also had the opportunity to work closely in the African National Congress Youth League (ANCYL) with the firebrand Africanists and lawyers Anton Muzwake Lembede and Robert Mangaliso Sobukwe. He also came under the influence of decolonial Afro-Marxists like Moses Kotane and William Nkomo. It was Lembede who declared that:

> it was an illusion of demented political demagogues to imagine that African workers as such can achieve their emancipation and reach their goal of being recognized by the government on the same footing with European trade unions while the rest of the African nation is still in chains and bondage of segregation, oppression, and colour discrimination. (Quoted in Halisi 1999: 64)

While Lembede and Sobukwe articulated the decolonization struggle from the perspective of radical Africanism, Kotane expressed a well-thought-out Afro-Marxist philosophy of liberation. In his letter of 1943, Kotane called for Africanization (which he termed 'bolshevization') of the South African Communist Party (SACP):

> Our party has and is suffering owing to being too Europeanized. If one investigates the general ideology of our party members (especially the whites), he will not fail to see that they subordinated South Africa in the interest of Europe. There are foreigners who know nothing about and who are least interested in the country in which they are living. But we are living in culturally backward Africa – Africa is economically and culturally backward. In Europe self-consciousness (class) has developed immensely whilst here national oppression, discrimination and exploitation confuses the class war and the majority of the African working population are more national conscious than class conscious. My first suggestion is that the party become Africanized, that we speak the language of the native masses and must know their demands. That while it must not lose its international allegiance, the party must be Bolshevized, become South African, not only theoretically but in reality, and not a party of a group of Europeans who are merely interested in European affairs. (South African Communist Party 1985: 120–22)

The main point that is missing in the existing biographies and hagiographies of Mandela is that his decolonial humanism emerged from the very crucible of deep colonial/racial oppression, the realities of racial proleterianization and practices of institutionalized racism. Mandela also makes it clear that he was also influenced by chieftaincy and the church during his early life:

The two influences that dominated my thoughts and actions during those days were chieftaincy and the church. After all, the only heroes I had heard of at that time had almost all been chiefs and the respect enjoyed by the regent from both black and white tended to exaggerate the importance of this institution in my mind ... Equally important was the position of the church, which I associated not so much with the body and doctrine contained in the Bible but with the person of Reverend Matyolo. (Mandela 2010: 11–12)

Mandela's move to Johannesburg and his stay in Alexandra introduced him to urban life: 'Here I learnt to adjust myself to urban life and came into physical contact with all the evils of white supremacy' (ibid.: 35). In Johannesburg, Mandela 'was introduced to various strands of thought' (ibid.: 43). But it was in the Communist Party meetings that Mandela 'found Europeans, Indians and Coloureds and Africans together' (ibid.: 44). One is led to argue that the Communist Party meetings symbolized the possibilities of a multi-racial society in which people of different races would live together as common citizens and enjoy equality.

While there are no direct connections between some early white liberals, like Olive Cronwright Schreiner, and the Mandela phenomenon, it is interesting to take note of some congruence between how they envisioned an inclusive South Africanism with that of Mandela. In fact the ANC and Mandela had to embrace the liberal, Marxist and nationalist interpretations of the South African problem into a broad Charterist movement in the 1950s. Schreiner was preoccupied with how to resolve the complex racial and ethnic identities that had formed at the southern tip of Africa. This is how she understood identity mix:

If a crude and homely illustration may be allowed, the peoples of South Africa resemble the constituents of a plum pudding when in the process of being mixed; the plums, the peel, the currants, the flour, the egg and the water are mingled together. Here plums may predominate, there the peel; one part may be slightly thinner than another, but it is useless to try and resort them; they have permeated each other's substance: they cannot be reseparated; to cut off a part would not be to resort them; it would be dividing a complex but homogenous substance into parts which would repeat its complexity. What then shall be said of the South African problem as a whole?

Is it impossible for the South African people to attain to any form of unity, organization, and normal life? Must we forever remain a vast, inchoate, invertebrate mass of humans, divided horizontally into layers of race, mutually antagonistic, and vertically severed by lines of political state division, which cut up our races without simplifying our problems, and which add to the bitterness of race conflict the irritation of political divisions? Is national life and organization unattainable by us? ... We believe that no one can impartially study the condition of South Africa and feel that it is so. Impossible as it is that our isolated states should consolidate and attain to a complete national life, there is a form of organic union which is possible to us. For there is a sense in which all South Africans are one ... there is [a] subtle but very real bond which unites all South Africans, and differentiates us from all other people in the world. This bond is our mixture of races itself. It is this which divides South Africa from all other peoples in the world, and makes us one. (Schreiner 1923: 60–61)

This is one early liberal reflection on the idea of South Africanism. The connection perhaps is that at the centre of the Mandela phenomenon pulsated the problem of constructing an inclusive South Africanism that was imbued with humanism as opposed to racism. Schreiner presented and understood the challenge this way:

If our view be right, the problem which South Africa has before it today is this: How from our political states and our discordant races, can a great, healthy, united, organized nation be formed? ... Our race question is complicated by a question of colour, which presents itself to us in a form more virulent and intense than that in which it has met any modern people. (Schreiner 1923: 62–64)

On the future of South Africa, Schreiner just like Mandela imagined a multiracial nation created by South Africans:

Our South African national structure in the future will not and cannot be identical with that of any other people, our national origin being so wholly unlike that of any other; our social polity must be developed by ourselves through the interaction of our parts with one another and in harmony with our complex needs. For good or evil, the South African nation will be an absolutely new thing under the sun, perhaps, owing to its mixture of races, possessing that strange vitality and originality which appears to rise so often from the mixture of human varieties: perhaps, in general human advance, ranking higher than other societies more simply constructed; perhaps lower, according as we shall shape it; but this, certainly, will be a new entity, with new problems, new gifts, new failings, new accomplishments. (Schreiner 1923: 370)

The African National Congress (ANC) that Mandela joined in the 1940s was basically a school for decolonial humanism, and was blessed with visionary decolonial humanists such as Pixley ka Seme, the founder of the ANC, and Chief Albert Luthuli, a president of the ANC and Nobel Peace Prize winner. Inevitably Mandela's ideological mind was watered from different political springs, all carrying in various degrees decolonial humanism that radiated at the very roots of the ANC itself. Seme was committed to the African struggle that was going to deliver a new civilization that was deeply humanistic. This is how he expressed his decolonial humanistic vision: 'The regeneration of Africa means that a new and unique civilization is soon to be added to the world ... The most essential departure of this new civilization is that it shall be thoroughly spiritual and humanistic – indeed a regeneration, moral and eternal!' (Seme 1906). On the other hand, Luthuli spoke of a broader decolonized civilizational African future as an African gift to the world. During his acceptance of the Nobel Prize, Luthuli informed the world that Africa was offering the world the gift of *ubuntu*, and proceeded to anticipate and envision a new post-racial civilization. His acceptance speech included this prediction: 'Somewhere ahead there beckons a civilization which will take its place in God's history with other great human syntheses: Chinese, Egyptian, Jewish, European. It will not necessarily be all black: but it will be African' (Luthuli 1961).

Mandela is a direct ideological descendent of this ANC decolonial humanism. Understood from this vantage point, a broader canvas is opened that places Mandela at the centre of a broader decolonial critique of the modernity/imperiality/coloniality/apartheid system. The same challenge of creating a peaceful and inclusive post-racial nation moved Thabo Mbeki, as deputy president of South Africa, to also reflect poetically on the meaning of inclusive South Africanism during the adoption of the South Africa constitution in 1996. This is how he articulated the content and form of South Africanism as an emergent historical African identity:

**23**

I owe my being to Khoi and the San ... I am formed of migrants who left Europe to find a new home on our native land ... In my veins courses the blood of the Malay slaves who came from the East. Their proud dignity informs my bearing, their culture a part of my essence ... I am the grandchild of the warrior men and women that Hintsa and Sekhukhune led, the patriots that Cetshwayo and Mphephu took to battle, the soldiers Moshoeshoe and Ngungunyane taught never to dishonour the cause of freedom ... I am the grandchild who lays fresh flowers on the Boer graves at St Helena and the Bahamas ... I come from those who were transported from India and China ... Being part of all these people and in the knowledge that one dare contest that assertion, I shall claim that I am an African. (Mbeki 1996: 31–36)

Mandela's political struggles as encapsulated in the autobiography, and as demonstrated in actual leadership of the ANC during Convention for a Democratic South Africa (CODESA) as well as his presidency, collectively signified a consistent push for decolonial turn, which Maldonado-Torres (2008b: 8) articulated as including 'the definitive entry of enslaved and colonized subjectivities into the realm of thought at previously unknown institutional levels'. Mbeki's speech is also a typical example of how to articulate this definitive entry and cannot be read in isolation from the broader canvas of the Mandela phenomenon.

The broad conceptual premise of this book is in tandem with Maldonado-Torres's argument (2008b: 8) that '[i]f the problem of the twentieth century and indeed the problem of modernity is the problem of the color line, the solution for the twentieth and twenty-first centuries is, at least in part, the decolonial turn' (see also Du Bois 1903). Mandela in this case is studied as the voice, conscience and representative of the enslaved, colonized and dehumanized subjectivities that have since the time of colonial encounters been fighting for restoration of their lost ontological density and for a new post-racial pluriversal world.

## Mandela as a Typical Decolonial Humanist

On his release from prison on 11 February 1990, Mandela greeted his supporters in a particularly revealing way, capturing the core aspects of decolonial humanism: 'I greet you all in the *name of peace, democracy and freedom for all! I stand before you as a humble servant of you, the people*' (my emphasis). This statement encapsulated what Enrique Dussel (2008: xvi) termed exercising 'obedential power' (command by obeying), founded on principles of politics as 'vocation' and an expression of the 'will to live' rather than the 'will to power'. When Mandela presented himself as 'a humble servant of the people' he was announcing a new conception of politics in which the exercise of power is not for the self but rather on behalf of the people.

Dussel (2008: 24) made a clear distinction between 'politics as vocation' and politics as 'bureaucratic profession'. As a vocation, politics is motivated by ideals and values with a strong 'normative content that inspires the subjectivity of the political actor towards a responsibility to the other, to the people' (ibid.). Politics as 'bureaucratic profession' is motivated by a will to power where the exercise of power is for individual gain. Mandela is one of those politicians that practised politics as vocation – a calling to fulfil a decolonial humanist mission. This explains why Anthony Sampson in *Mandela: The Authorized Biography* (1999: 87) noted that '[d]espite Mandela's political evolution, he still retained his basic African nationalism: his pride in his people and their history, and his determination to regain their rights'.

Mandela can best be described as a radical African nationalist-liberal-decolonial humanist who dedicated his life to a struggle against racism, imperialism, colonialism and apartheid. Racism, the slave trade, imperialism, colonialism, apartheid, neo-colonialism and underdevelopment have all existed as the underbelly of Euro-North American-centric modernity since 1492. When Mandela was released from prison in 1990 he knew that his supporters were much too thirsty for peace, democracy, liberation and freedom after enduring over 350 years of multiple forms of oppression. Apartheid colonialism had robbed black people of dignity and humanity itself. Mandela emerges as an uncompromising historian and a champion of decolonial humanism, and his political thought cannot be ignored in the present-day search for decolonial-liberatory modern political theory.

Decolonial humanism is a long-standing struggle for life spearheaded by those the oppressed people exposed to the negative consequences of modernity. These are people who have been pushed by global imperial designs to live in the 'zone of non-being'. In the 'zone of non-being' there is a scarcity of humanism and life itself. Peace, democracy, liberation and freedom, as constituents of life and humanism, are absent in this 'zone of non-being'. Mandela dedicated his life to the epic African nationalist-humanist decolonial struggle for peace, democracy and freedom. A biographical approach to understand Mandela's life of struggle with its proclivity towards celebrations and eulogies is inadequate to the task of capturing the various meanings of Mandela.

Decolonial humanism is opposed to the paradigm of war and racism, and is committed to the advancement of the unfinished and ongoing project of decolonization as a precondition for the paradigm of peace and post-racial pluriversal humanism. Therefore, a critical decolonial ethical study of Mandela's life of struggle and legacy inevitably enables a critical engagement with the broader question of the meaning and essence of being human (subject, subjection, subjectivity, resistance and liberation) and conditions that inhibited the human flourishing, in this case the paradigm of war and apartheid. Decolonial humanism is preoccupied with two fundamental questions that were clearly posed by the leading African philosopher Emmanuel Chukwudi Eze in his book *Achieving Our Humanity: The Idea of the Postracial Future*:

> How would an African or black person anywhere think about the world – the global modern world which thinks of 'blacks' as a race – beyond the idea of race but without denying the fact that racial identities and racism are important aspects of the modern experience? In what ways could one transcend the race-conscious traditions of both modern European and African thought which sustain ideologies of race and racism while recognizing that there are in these intellectual traditions powerful tools against racialism and racism? (Eze 2001: ix)

This book challenges the paradigm of war as the normal state of human life and Slavoj Zizek's intervention that Mandela's iconic status and 'universal glory is also a sign that he really didn't disturb the global order of power' (Zizek 2013: 1). This is a common critique that cascades from those analysts and thinkers who focus on Mandela the person to the extent of missing the bigger picture of Mandela as an idea, a voice and a representative of a broader decolonial utopic imaginary. This type of critique also minimizes the challenges and sensitivities cascading from global and local circles that needed careful negotiation and navigation before placing South Africa on a new post-apartheid platform of 'freedom to be free' as Mandela put it.

There is no doubt that Mandela deployed principles of critical decolonial ethics of liberation to question and challenge the modernity/imperial/colonial/apartheid paradigm of war and racial hatred directly. What is the subject of debate is how successful he was in changing this paradigm. Mandela's uniqueness lies in his advocacy of a paradigm of peace informed by a full commitment to democracy and human rights, to racial harmony, to racial reconciliation, and to post-racial pluriversalism as part of his contribution to speaking the truth to a Euro-North American-centric world system that continues to be resistant to decolonization, and its shifting global orders that continue to be impervious to deimperialization.

## Contestations over Meaning and Legacy of Mandela

Contestations over the meaning of Mandela and his legacy is broadly part of the contestations over the idea of South Africa and the concomitant questions of the nation, belonging, citizenship, democracy and the meaning of liberation. Mandela is one of those leading African decolonial humanists and political leaders who consistently tried to learn 'to live within the conceptual purgatory of race and class interpretations of liberation politics' (Halisi 1999: 12), and who eventually took a pragmatic and synthetic position on the idea of South Africa, the essence of the nation, criteria of citizenship and democracy, to the celebration of some and the chagrin of others. Sarah Nuttall and Achille Mbembe captured the complexities of the idea of South Africa and the place of Mandela in it when they wrote:

> We examine the pervasive feeling in South Africa that Mandela's death might reveal a void at the centre of a country that has always tried to mask such an emptiness at its centre: a country that has struggled to define itself as a nation and draw together its many fragments into a sustained sense of commonality in the wake of a long racist past. More than anybody else, Mandela embodied this sense of commonality, and his passing is likely to reignite the metaphysical anxiety that South Africa is neither a concept nor an idea – just a place, a geographical accident. (Nuttall and Mbembe 2014: 268)

Mandela, who turned out to be the pivot of the imagined post-apartheid nation, could not escape being open to all sorts of contestations. At one level, Mandela's life of struggle and legacy became caught up in what C.R.D. Halisi articulated as the liberal versus the republican traditions: 'Forged in the crucible of racial oppression, black political thought fluctuates incessantly between the values of racial autonomy and interracial social incorporation' (Halisi 1999: 1). In reality, 'the conquest and proletarianization have produced powerful traditions of racial populism that are woven into the very fabric of political discourse' (ibid.: 20). Mandela had to swallow all this, digest it, synthesize it, and rearticulate it in a more inclusive manner.

Inevitably, within South Africa, Mandela's legacy is a subject of intense contestation among political gladiators. The political campaign for the national elections that took place on 7 May 2014 witnessed unprecedented struggles and contestations over who and which political party represented Mandela's legacy and embodied his spirit of life of struggle. Despite the fact that Mandela died as a member of the ruling African National Congress and had even vowed to open an ANC branch 'in heaven', the organization came under immense pressure to claim and monopolize Mandela. Since his death on 5 December 2013, and even during his lifetime, such political formations as the Congress of the People (COPE) and the Democratic Alliance (DA) have also been trying to claim a piece of Mandela as they criticized the ANC for betraying his legacy.

The ANC and the South African Communist Party (SACP) have responded by trying to keep Mandela tightly as the soul and property of the ANC, inviting voters to continue voting for Mandela through the ANC even after his death. Even the recently formed Economic Freedom Fighters (EFF) led by Julius Malema are claiming Mandela as their inspiration. Malema said, 'We are inspired by President Nelson Mandela himself, the real Nelson Mandela, not the artificial one that you guys have created for yourself' (Malema in the *City Press*, 22 April 2014).

This jostling over the Mandela legacy cannot be simplistically dismissed as political gimmicks deployed by political gladiators to win elections. It indicates that Mandela meant different things to different people, and those things are evaluated positively across the political ideological divide. The Mandela phenomenon spoke to a future that has not yet been reached – the future as potentiality, possibility, and a space to create new forms of sociality beyond race and racism. The previously mentioned recent work of Rita Barnard, *The Cambridge Companion to Nelson Mandela*, does not fully capture the global meanings of Mandela. Rather it approaches Mandela as an ordinary political figure who was besieged by numerous antinomies as part of trying to penetrate beyond the iconic figure, including exposing how Mandela struggled to synthesize the tensions between tradition and modernity as well as his supposed oscillation between Africanist and nonracial positions. It concludes with a postcolonial meditation on Mandela's legacy and the future without him.

The current book broadens the debate on the meaning of the Mandela phenomenon while at the same time highlighting the global and local context within which it crystallized and assumed different meanings. Mandela actively worked towards dismantling the institutionalized racism that was known as apartheid. But apartheid was part of a global problem that had permeated into the minds of South Africans just like all other colonial systems. Decolonizing the minds of the people who have experienced long periods of colonization, apartheid and now coloniality, becomes a lengthy if not lifetime undertaking. By the time of his death, Mandela had still not succeeded in undoing the socio-economic inequalities that were deliberately created under apartheid. Should we therefore dismiss Mandela as a tragic hero who delivered nothing? The South African black consciousness political activist Andile Mngxitama (2008: 1) understands Mandela 'as South Africa's metaphor' of disappointment and 'a perfect embodiment of postcolonial Africa'. He elaborated that:

> Mandela is, in some way, a perfect embodiment of postcolonial Africa, a continent blessed with so many possibilities but consistently producing so much disappointment. The African dream of liberation has become a long nightmare. As Mandela turns 90, the country he helped found some 14 years ago is in a mighty mess. Its hatred of black people has reached the apex with the mass slaughtering and displacement of black Africans. Post-1994 has been much celebrated for the benefits it bestowed upon a few; silence has befallen the fate of the black majority which has been bequeathed a bestial existence. (Mngxitama 2008: 1)

This reading of Mandela as a failure is pronounced among some black constituencies that have not seen a qualitative change in their socio-economic life since the transition from apartheid to democracy. This is a constituency that is seething with anger emanating from an expectation crisis. It is this constituency that interpreted Mandela as 'a euphemism or code for deference, patience, forgiveness, reconciliation and absolute love of whites' rather than for humanity in general (More [no date]: 8). This reading of Mandela sees him as having been disciplined by long imprisonment to the extent of undergoing metamorphosis from a radical decolonial nationalist to a highly compromised neoliberal who abandoned the politics of nationalization of the commanding heights of the economy as documented in the Freedom Charter of 1955. Those who push this argument go to the extent of describing Mandela as a sell out. It is a charge that is levelled at Mandela mainly by the unemployed youth who are deeply disappointed by the transition from apartheid to democracy. Mandela is said to have failed to deliver economic freedom. He is said to have presided over profoundly compromised CODESA negotiations that produced 'an intra-elite economic deal of neo-colonialism' (Modisane 2014).

The frustration of the South African youth is understandable; but that Mandela was a sell out might be a sign of a failure to appreciate the complexity of the South African struggle and the challenge of dealing with an undefeated enemy. Zakes Mda's take might be helpful here:

> I understand the disillusionment of these young people, although I do not share their perspective. To me, Mandela was neither the devil they make him out to be nor the saint that most of my compatriots and the international community think he was. I see him as a skilful politician, smart enough to resist megalomania that comes with dei-fication. I don't think the policy of reconciliation was ill-advised; it saved the country from a bloodbath and ushered a period of prosper-ity. (Mda 2013: 1)

As I posited in the Preface, Mandela's struggle must be appreci-ated from a perspective of a decolonial civilizational project rather than of a narrow political economy. Mandela himself provides part of the answer to his critics:

> Only armchair politicians are immune from committing mistakes. Errors are inherent in political action. Those who are in the centre of political struggle, who have to deal with practical and pressing problems, are afforded little time for reflection and no precedents to guide them, and are bound to slip up many times. But in due course, and provided they are flexible and prepared to examine their work self critically, they will acquire the necessary experience and fore-sight that will enable them to avoid the ordinary pitfalls and pick out their way ahead amidst the throb of events. (Mandela 2010: 34)

The current book reveals the complexities of the South African struggle and the enormity of the issues and dangers that had to be navigated and negotiated to avoid the country falling into further bloodshed and chaos. It takes into account the changing post-Cold War global order and the pressures that were put on the ANC and Mandela from representatives of local and global capital that wanted post-apartheid South Africa to emerge as part of the neo-liberal dispensation. The unrepentant racists were threatening to plunge the nation into bloodshed so as to derail the transition from apartheid to democracy. A so-called black-on-black violence was being fomented and sponsored as part of a broader agenda of derailing the negotiations. Continuing the armed struggle was constrained by the collapse of the Soviet Union, which had sponsored the ANC. The available options for the negotiators from the liberation side were limited as they were dealing not only with an undefeated enemy but also a cunning and plotting force that still wanted to maintain white dominance.

I must say that writing about Mandela in the context of a complex struggle invokes the proverbial three blind people who were trying to describe an elephant. In this case, it is the broad decolonial civilizational project that needed the buy-in of the ex-colonized and the ex-colonizers alike. Depending on where the blind people were touching, they offered divergent descriptions of the animal. Thus, if the Mandela decolonial civilizational project has failed, it is not because it was wrong but because it lacked the genuine buy-in of ex-colonizers who took advantage of his decolonial magnanimity to reproduce the status quo of domination, racism and inequality. Further to this, such a broad decolonial civilizational struggle cannot be expected to be a mere epochal one; it is even more than a lifetime struggle as it is meant to reverse over five hundred years of Euro-North American-centric modernity/imperiality/coloniality architecture and configuration of power, being and knowledge predicated on race and a 'will to power'.

## Seeking to Understand the Mandela Phenomenon

While all biographies, hagiographies and flimologies of Mandela sought to understand him as a political actor – that is, as a person of exceptional qualities – this book is seeking to understand the Mandela phenomenon from a critical decolonial ethical perspective that goes beyond focusing on the Mandela as a person. Those who have studied Mandela and written on him before me, such as Raymond Suttner (2007) and Paul Maylam (2009), emphasized the complexity of the subject. Suttner is a stalwart of the liberation struggle who knew Mandela personally. Building on his personal knowledge of Mandela and the ANC, he criticized most of the biographers of Mandela for 'misunderstanding' him. Suttner posited that:

To understand Mandela, and especially as a political figure, it is essential to locate him as a changing political and human being in a dynamic and diverse political environment. In particular, how the ANC works, how it alters its mode of operating, the extent to which even a powerful personality like Mandela is constrained by this organization, must be understood. (Suttner 2007: 110)

Suttner elaborated that those who wished to understand Mandela have to read 'Mandela in the ANC' not outside the ANC; the complexity is compounded by the fact that the ANC 'is both the same and different' affected by 'continuities and raptures'. Following the argument of Suttner, if one missed the interrelationship between Mandela and the ANC, there was the danger of misreading 'Mandela as a political being who himself changes overtime'. He also admitted that there were times when Mandela's popularity far exceeded that of the ANC, sometimes giving him opportunities to 'act without organizational authority' (Suttner 2007: 110). Interestingly though, Suttner also revealed that Mandela always respected other leaders such as Moses Kotane and Walter Sisulu to the extent of deferring to them. This is how he put it:

> The primary relationship between Sisulu and Mandela was always one in which Sisulu would be in the background and Mandela would be in the overt leadership position. But deference to Sisulu's understanding and judgment is a constant theme of their interaction. (Suttner 2007: 112)

More than the question of organizational authority, Suttner also ascribed primacy to settling the question of Mandela's ideological orientation. He noted that some works on Mandela tried frantically to 'fit him into a specific political orientation', with some calling him a liberal and others debating whether Mandela was ever a communist, Marxist, or a Gandhist who was opposed to the use of violence in the liberation struggle (Suttner 2007: 119–23). He outrightly dismissed the idea of Mandela being a Gandhist as inapplicable. On Mandela being a liberal, Suttner (ibid.: 120) pointed out that he 'agreed with representative democracy, which is not the exclusive property of liberalism'. The important point that emerges from Suttner's analysis is that Mandela appropriated various local and global ideological resources as a leader of the

ANC in an effort 'to rally support from all quarters, especially those that had been hostile or indifferent to the struggle of the ANC. It was part of his mission to win them over to support the organization' (ibid.: 121).

In this, Suttner was correct to emphasize that, in writing about Mandela, one was 'dealing with a complex life that deserves more in-depth exploration' (2007: 128). Maylam (2009) adopted two approaches to understand Mandela. The first one was built on the work of John Campbell (1949) on heroes with many faces. Following this work, Maylam explored how Mandela could be understood as an archetypal hero. Archetypal heroes had a clear trajectory of separation, initiation and return to society. With Mandela, this trajectory would fit the Rivonia Trial and imprisonment as representing separation of Mandela from society; the long imprisonment as the political initiation; and the release from prison as the return of a saviour-like figure (Maylam 2009: 35–36). But Maylam found this articulation of Mandela akin to reducing him to a 'semi-mythical figure'. He therefore preferred an approach that emphasized Mandela's humanism founded on principles of 'humility, integrity, generosity of spirit, and wisdom' that were opposed to the negative attributes of 'grandiosity, ostentation and personality cults' (ibid.: 36).

This book is a study of the Mandela phenomenon as underpinned by profound humanism. It is a critical decolonial reflective perspective, which like all other perspectives is limited and provisional. I hope the reflections contained in this book will be taken as worthwhile contemplations of the Mandela phenomenon and that they will be taken as they are – that is, as personal and partial reflections on an important subject and an important African leader. Like all other reflections, they are an invitation to broader interdisciplinary conversations on the Mandela phenomenon beyond the scope of biographies and hagiographies.

# One

# Decolonial Theory of Life

## Introduction

> This then is what the ANC is fighting for. Their struggle is a truly national one.
>
> It is a struggle of the African people, inspired by their own suffering and their own experience. It is a struggle for the right to live.
> – Nelson Mandela, *Long Walk to Freedom*

> I have walked that long road to freedom. I have tried not to falter. I have made missteps along the way. But I have discovered the secret that after climbing a hill, one only finds that there are many more hills to climb. I have taken a moment here to rest, to steal a view of the glorious vista that surrounds me, to look back on the distance I have come. But I can rest only for a moment, for with freedom comes responsibilities, and I dare not linger, for my long walk is not yet ended.
> – Nelson Mandela, *Long Walk to Freedom*

The decolonial theory of life is founded on the 'will to live' rather that the 'will to power'. It is fundamentally a decolonial humanistic expression that is opposed to the paradigm of war linked to coloniality. Nelson Rolihlahla Mandela was a living expression of the decolonial theory of life. This is why the Nigerian Nobel Laureate Wole Soyinka (2006: 24) characterized Mandela 'as

**35**

humanistic expression'. Indeed if Mandela was an expression of decolonial humanism and his life of struggle was for a new politics of life, then the African National Congress (ANC) was a decolonial political school and a site of political socialization of decolonial humanists, beginning with such leaders as Pixley ka Isaka Seme, Langalibalele Dube and Albert Luthuli. Even Mandela himself had to learn a lot from this decolonial school where narrow Africanism and reserve racism had to be transcended, and new decolonial humanist ideals and ethics, and gesturing towards the creation of an inclusive, non-racial, non-sexist, democratic and post-apartheid society were inculcated. Mandela was well aware of the ANC as a school: 'I matured politically within the ranks of a movement and a leadership that were critical in shaping my outlook' (quoted in Sampson 1999: 495). These pluriversal ideals and others that were socialist-oriented were well captured in the Freedom Charter of 1955. The ANC as a school is also captured well in *Nelson Mandela: Conversations with Myself*, in which Mandela specifically wrote:

> I was twenty-one then and my subsequent association with the African National Congress and progressive ideas helped me to crawl out of the prejudice of my youth and to accept all people as equals. I came to accept that I have no right whatsoever to judge others in terms of my own customs, however much I may be proud of such customs; that to despise others because they have not observed particular customs is a dangerous form of chauvinism. (Mandela 2010: 26)

A decolonial school is against all fundamentalisms and egoisms. The ANC's ideology of racial inclusivity and equality is typically decolonial. The ANC decolonial political school made Mandela fully aware of challenges that faced and affected those who were committed to the decolonial struggle:

> My association with the African National Congress has taught me that a broad national movement has numerous and divergent contradictions, fundamental and otherwise. The presence in one organization of various classes and social groups with conflicting long-term interests many collide at crucial moments, and brings its own conflicts. (Mandela 2010: 26)

Because decoloniality is against all forms of fundamentalisms and egocentrisms, it enabled the ANC to easily become a home to socialists, liberals and Africanists as long as they all were committed to the decolonial struggle. While the socialist ideals lost some favour in the 1990s following the collapse of the Soviet Union and the implosion of socialist regimes in Eastern Europe, other pluriversal ideals gained a further boost from the globalization process that was accompanied by denationalization and deterritorialization processes. The current leadership of the ANC, despite numerous criticisms, have vowed to continue the decolonial humanist struggle, building from where Mandela left off. All those from the Global South who have walked through the shadow of death and experienced and survived the devastating effects of the imperial/colonial/apartheid paradigm of war are still fighting for new humanism and a paradigm of peace. Mandela fought for the life of those who were consigned by global imperial designs to the category of 'the wretched of the earth'.

## Beyond Hellenocentrism, Westernization and Eurocentrism

Mandela's decolonial humanist struggle was aimed at creating another civilization beyond the exclusivist modern world shaped by forces of Hellenocentrism, Westernization, Eurocentrism, imperial reason, and the paradigm of war. This is a world bereft of humanism. Therefore, at the centre of Mandela's life of struggle and legacy, one finds a very deep and profound humanism as the driving force of his political actions. One cannot therefore understand the Mandela phenomenon without deploying decoloniality as a theory of life. Decoloniality is a theory of life in the sense that it is founded on the need to decolonize being, to decolonize knowledge, and to decolonize power, which are imbricated in denial of life to those who were pushed into the zone of non-being.

'Being' was colonized through racial profiling, classification, and hierarchization of the human population. Knowledge was colonized through epistemicides and appropriations of other knowledges while pretending that the only valid knowledge came from Europe and North America. Power was colonized in various ways including usurpation if not theft of world history and its rearticulation through the prism of Hellenocentrism, Eurocentrism and Westernization. Decolonial theory is therefore ranged against various epistemological, ideological, political and social projects and processes imposed on the modern world by Euro-North American-centric modernity after 1492. The leading philosopher of liberation, Enrique Dussel (2011: xv), clearly identified the core contours of usurpation of world history by Europeans. The first process he termed 'Hellenocentrism', which laid the foundation for Eurocentrism. Hellenocentrism instantiated that: 'All start in Greece'. This Euro-North American-centric and egocentric conception of human history resulted in what the leading African historian Paul Tiyambe Zeleza (1997) termed the 'Athens-to-Washington' historiographical narrative, which privileged Greece (in particular Athens) as the beginning of human civilization. Hellenocentrism gave birth to Westernization as a process of imposing Euro-North American-centric values on other people accompanied by the displacement of some values and the expropriation of others. This is why the Peruvian sociologist Anibal Quijano articulated the inscription of coloniality of power in these revealing words:

> The repression fell, above all, over the modes of knowing, of producing knowledge, of producing perspectives, images and systems of images, symbols, modes of signification, over the resources, patterns and instruments of formalized and objectivised expression, intellectual or visual. It was followed by the imposition of the use of the rulers' own patterns of expression, and of their beliefs and images with reference to the supernatural ... The colonizers also imposed a mystified image of their own patterns of producing knowledge and meaning. At first, they placed these patterns far out of reach of the dominated. Later, they taught them in a partial and selective way, in order to co-opt some of the dominated into their own power institutions. Then European culture was made seductive: it gave access to power. After all, beyond repression, the main instrument of all power is its seduction ... European culture became a universal cultural model. The imaginary in the non-European cultures could

hardly exist today and, above all, reproduce itself outside of these relations. (Quijano 2007: 169)

In this articulation of human history, the United States of America (Washington) is the beacon of human civilizational achievement. Jack Goody in his *The Theft of History* (2006) presents the centrality of Europe in human history as predicated on 'theft of history'. This is how he put it:

> The 'theft of history' ... refers to the takeover of history by the West. That is, the past is conceptualized and presented according to what happened on the provincial scale of Europe, often Western Europe, and then imposed upon the rest of the world. That continent makes many claims to having invented a range of value-laden institutions such as 'democracy', mercantile 'capitalism', freedom, individualism. (Goody 2006: 1)

At the centre of Westernization was an epistemological process of claiming knowledge as an artefact of Western societies. Westernization was driven by 'Eurocentrism', which 'is the label for all the beliefs that postulate past or present superiority of Europeans over non-Europeans (and over minority people of non-European descent) (Blaut 1993: 8). According to Dussel (2011: xvi), Eurocentrism was propelled by a deliberate forgetting 'through disdain and ignorance of everything that was achieved by other cultures, practically, politically and theoretically'. One of the most debated consequences of Eurocentrism is what the Palestinian scholar Edward Said (1978) described as 'orientalism' – a shorthand of the West's historical, cultural and political perceptions of the East. Eurocentrism resulted in routinization of global binary that the Nigerian decolonial thinker Chinweizu (1975) elucidated as 'the west and the rest of us'. The implications and consequences of Eurocentrism are well documented by James M. Blaut in *The Colonizer's Model of the World: Geographical Diffusion and Eurocentric History* (1993). The first was that Europe (the West) has had some unique historical advantage including special racial qualities that gave it 'a permanent superiority over all other communities'. The second was that Europeans are the makers of human history. The third was that Europe is positioned on an eternal state of human advancement, progression and modernization, while other parts of the world are stagnant and traditional. The final was that 'Europe is the source of most diffusion; non-Europe is the recipient' (Blaut 1993: 1).

The leading Egyptian economist Samir Amin (2009: 34) understood Eurocentrism as 'the great ideological deformations of our time'. What were deformed by Eurocentrism were ideas concerning the human itself. Europeans claimed 'being' for themselves and assigned 'becoming' for others (Ndlovu-Gatsheni 2013c). Taken together, these processes resulted in imperial reason that claimed secularism and rationality as its well spring but remaining deeply racist. Decoloniality as a theory of life invites all of us to 'learn to discover new questions in order to encounter new answers' (Dussel 2011: xviii). Decoloniality is against denial if not destruction of other people's ontological densities, resulting in such people being physically pushed out of the human ocumene. Decoloniality is founded on the will to live not the will to power.

## From the Will to Power to the Will to Live

The dawn of Euro-North American-centric modernity universalized the will to power as the natural leitmotif of politics. This will to power enabled the naturalization of war, which was informed by what Dussel described as 'fetishism of power'.

> [This] consists of the moment in which the political actor (the member of the political community, whether citizens or representatives) believes that power affirms his or her subjectivity or the institution in which he or she functions – as a 'functionary', whether it be as president, representative, judge, governor, soldier, police officer – as the centre or source of political power. (Dussel 2008: 4)

The fetishism of power unfolded in terms of corruption of what Dussel (2008: xv) termed the 'noble vocation of politics'. This was founded on the will to live, but corrupted into the will to power. This is described by Dussel (ibid.: 4) as the 'originary corruption of the political', and is the first of Dussel's 'twenty theses on politics'. According to Dussel:

The fetishization of power ... consists of a 'Will-to-Power, as domination of the people, of the majority, of the weakest, of the poor. All other definitions must be rejected as idealistic, insufficiently realistic, moralistic, and ineffective. In this case, politics is the art of exercising power over antagonists who are subjected – at best, hegemonically – to the will of fetishized institutions in favour of some particular members of the community. (ibid.: 33)

Western classical philosophers beginning with those from ancient Greece such as Heraclitus, have been mobilized in the crusade to inscribe the paradigm of war as a natural feature of human life. In this paradigm of war, human beings are defined as 'homo polemos' (warrior, war-maker) whose humanity cascades from 'I kill, therefore I am' (Sonderling 2012: 49). Ramon Grosfoguel summarized the logic of the paradigm of war in a dramatic manner:

During the last 510 years of capitalist/patriarchal western-centric, Christian-centric, modern-colonial system we went from the 16th century 'Christianize or I shoot you', to the 19th century 'civilize or I shoot you', to 20th century 'develop or I shoot you,' to late 20th century 'neo-liberalize or I shoot you', to the early 21st century 'democratize or I shoot you'. (Grosfoguel 2011: 20)

This naturalization of the paradigm of war is a central theme of Western tradition of thought. For instance Thomas Hobbes (1958) popularized the idea that the original state of nature was a condition of permanent war in which life was short, nasty and brutish. Such classical works as Charles Darwin's *The Origins of Species* ([1879] 2011) were easily appropriated by advocates of the paradigm of war to give it an evolutionary-biological basis. Darwin's concept of the 'survival of the fittest' became useful in the work of later Social Darwinists who pushed forward the imperial agenda of scientific racism.

Indeed Darwin might have been innocently using his knowledge as a naturalist to advance frontiers of scientific knowledge beyond religiously informed explanations of the origins of people, but his work was easily appropriated and mobilized to back up the paradigm of war, including imperialism, colonialism and apartheid. In the paradigm of war, slavery and the slave trade are justified as normal and natural. It is part of Nietzsche's meditations on the practice of the will to power. Even the celebrated Marxist conception of human history as constituted by class struggles has a notion of a paradigm of war at its centre. In short, the paradigm of war enabled imperialism, colonialism and apartheid. It is the paradigm of war that was and is at the heart of the arms race and the production of deadly nuclear weapons today. The present scourge of global terrorism is informed by the paradigm of war. In short, the paradigm of war constituted the leitmotif of Euro-North American-centric modernity. Its naturalization benefited from the fact that one of Euro-North American-centric modernity's successes has been the naturalization of the unnatural. Not only was the paradigm of war naturalized, but also an attendant racial hierarchization of being.

The paradigm of peace that was embodied by Mandela did not emerge from the Euro-North American world, where inordinate efforts were spent on naturalizing the paradigm of war. The paradigm of peace is genealogically traceable to those people who became victims to the paradigm of war. They include those who experienced the slave trade in the first instance, and those who have since experienced racialization. These became victims not only of the slave trade, but also of imperialism, colonialism, apartheid, neo-colonialism and underdevelopment. What analysts from the Global South ought to avoid is buying into the Western tradition of thought that worked hard to naturalize the paradigm of war. Those people from the Global South have experienced the devastating effects of the naturalized paradigm of war and must vehemently reject it as a feature of human society. It is therefore important to understand human trajectory from a liberating decolonial humanist perspective because it enables one to see the fallacy of the naturality of the paradigm of war.

## Towards a Third Humanist Revolution

Understood from a decolonial humanist perspective, the human trajectory has already undergone two humanist revolutions and is currently experiencing a third one which is not yet complete. These shifts, which are diagrammatically expressed in Figure 1.1, can be

## Renaissance
- Shift from God-centered humanity
- Religion/theology

## Enlightenment
- Man-centered humanism
- Rationality/science

## Imperial Reason
- "I conquer, therefore I am."/*Homo polemos*
- Will to power
- Paradigm of war

## Cartesianism
- "I think, therefore I am."/Cogito ergo sum.
- Egocentrism/racism/sexism
- Knowledge/science/discovery

## European/North American-Centric Modernity
- Slavery/slave trade
- Mercantilism/imperialism/capitalism
- Colonialism/Christianisation/coloniality

## Decolonial Humanism
- Decolonisation/deimperialisation
- Paradigm of peace/human development/humanism
- Ubuntu / "I am because you are." / will to live

## Pluriversalism
- Co-humanness
- Many worlds in one
- Ecologies of knowledge

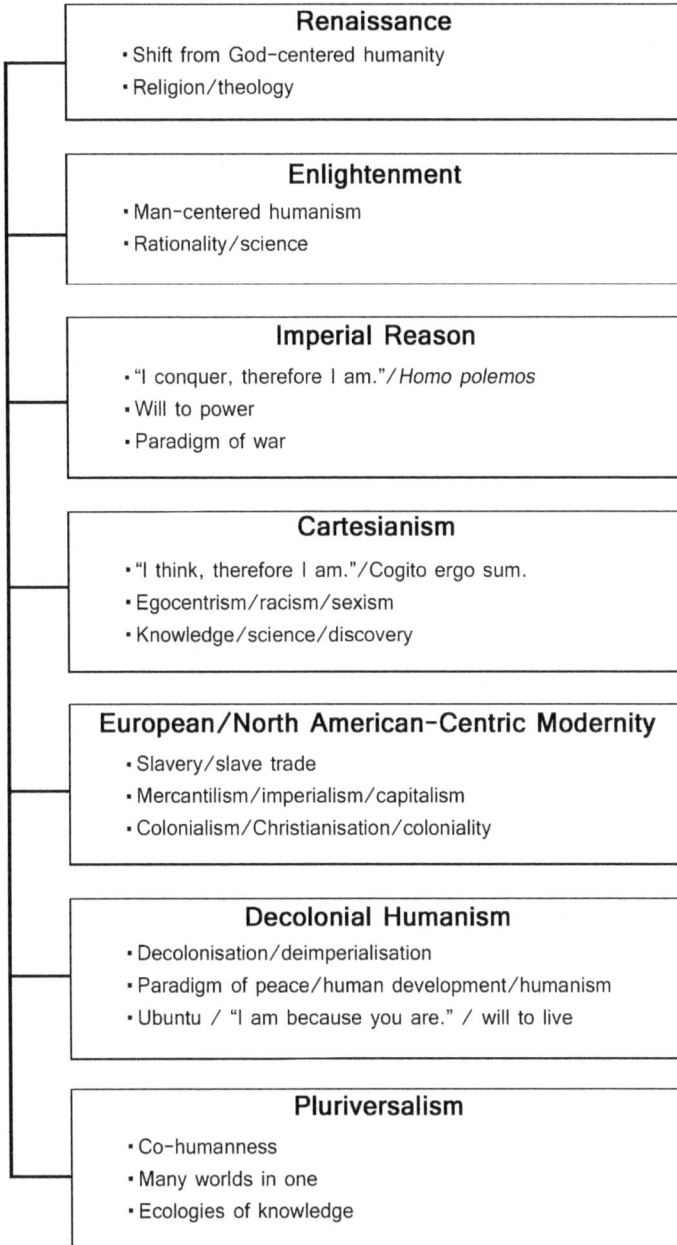

**Figure 1.1** Decolonial humanism.

documented as from God-centred conceptions of humanism that was challenged during the Renaissance to a Man-centred society that became ubiquitous during the age of Enlightenment. At the centre of this shift one can decipher particular philosophies such as the famous Cartesian notion of the cogito: 'I think, therefore I am' (Descartes 2013). According to Ramon Grosfoguel (2013: 75), Descartes' thought on being also constituted 'a new foundation of knowledge that challenged Christendom's authority of knowledge since the Roman Empire'. This was preceded by what Grosfoguel describes as 'I exterminate, therefore I am' that culminated in 'I conquer, therefore I am'. These two logics authorized what Grosfoguel (ibid.: 73–74) identified as the 'the four genocides/epistemicides of the long 16th century'.

These genocides/epistemicides took the historical-imperial form of conquest of Al-Andalusia involving the extermination of Jewish and Muslim people; the conquest of the Americas and the extermination of indigenous peoples; the kidnapping and enslavement of Africans; and the burning of books and white women in Indo-Europe who were accused of witchcraft (Grosfoguel 2013: 73–74). Imperial reason was feeding all these conceptions of Cartesian being. Imperial reason became the nerve centre of the paradigm of war. It was further boosted by Darwinian notions of the survival of the fittest and the proliferation of scientific racism in the nineteenth century.

## Beyond the Paradigm of War, Towards a Paradigm of Peace

A paradigm of war is defined as 'a way of conceiving humanity, knowledge, and social relations that privileges conflict or *polemos*' (Maldonado-Torres 2008b: 3). In his groundbreaking book *Against War*, the philosopher and decolonial theorist Maldonado-Torres articulated the core contours of the paradigm of war that are constitutive of 'coloniality'. Coloniality, which is defined in the Preface and prologue of this book, is genealogically traceable to the emergence Euro-North American-centric modernity in 1492, the date that decolonial theorists identified as figuratively marking the birth of the modern world system and its shifting global orders (Blaut 1993; Mignolo 1995, 2000, 2011; Quijano 2000; Grosfoguel 2007, 2011; Ndlovu-Gatsheni 2013a).

Christopher Columbus's breakthrough, which saw him accidentally reaching the Americas while trying to reach the East Indies and became known as the discovery of the 'New World' in imperial/colonial discourse, is interpreted by decolonial theorists as paradigmatic in a number of ways. In the first instance, it is said to have marked the birth of a world capitalist economy whose nerve centre was the Atlantic region. In the second instance, it opened the resources of Latin America to colonial exploitation by Europe. In the third instance, it marked the beginning of the rise of Europe and the crystallization of its notion of being the centre of the world. Taken together, these developments marked the birth of a peculiar Euro-North American-centric modernity and a new world system founded on racism (Blaut 1993; Mignolo 1995, 2000, 2011; Quijano 2000, 2007; Amin 2009; Ndlovu-Gatsheni 2013b, 2013c).

The rise of Euro-North American-centric modernity enabled the birth of modern subjectivity mediated by race as an organizing principle. A unique modernist consciousness that manifested itself in terms of a radical ontological unevenness between Euro-North Americans and non-Europeans emerged. A world system that Ramon Grosfoguel (2007, 2011) characterized as racially hierarchized, patriarchal, sexist, hetero-normative, Euro-North American-centric, Christian-centric, capitalist, imperial, colonial and modern was also born.

This world system was managed by what became known as Cartesian subjects (Euro-North American people) who had elevated themselves into a master race that was capable of using secular knowledge and science to overcome all obstacles to human happiness. These Cartesian subjects claimed 'being' for themselves and relegated all other people who were not of European stock and descent to the realm of 'becoming' human (Maldonado-Torres 2007; Grosfoguel 2007; Ndlovu-Gatsheni 2013b, 2013c). At the centre of this Euro-North American-centric world was what Maldonado-Torres (2007: 245) articulated as the 'imperial

Manichean misanthropic skepticism' that was naturalized through use of natural science to produce scientific racism. As elaborated by Maldonado-Torres: 'Manichean misanthropic skepticism is not skeptical about the existence of the world or the normative status of logics and mathematics. It is rather a form of questioning the very humanity of colonized peoples' (ibid.). Constitutively, the paradigm of war is fed by racism and is inextricably tied to 'a peculiar death ethic that renders massacre and different forms of genocide as natural' (Maldonado-Torres 2008b: xi).

Thus while the paradigm of war is traceable to the birth of Euro-North American-centric modernity and capitalism, the paradigm of peace originated in the Global South as an epistemic site in which the slave trade, imperialism, colonialism and apartheid were practised, contested and resisted. The paradigm of peace is informed by what Maldonado-Torres (2008a) has termed the third humanist revolution founded on the philosophy 'I am, because you are'. This is constitutive of decolonial humanism of which Mandela became a leading advocate in the twentieth and twenty-first centuries. But the paradigm of peace has a long pedigree.

It is traceable to such people as the ex-slaves, like Ottobah Cugoano who wrote *Thoughts on the Evils of Slavery and Other Writings* (1789), where he expressed his dismay at how Europeans who claimed to be Christians had embarked on the slave trade. The paradigm of peace is founded on what the philosopher, historian and theologian Enrique Dussel in his *Twenty Theses on Politics* (2008) described as the politics of life. Eduardo Mendieta (2008: viii) elaborated on what Dussel (1989, 2011) termed 'philosophy of liberation / politics of liberation', highlighting what he termed 'a politics of life with others and for others' and 'a politics of life and for life, a politics from the underside of necrophilic globalization'.

Mandela was not the first leader emerging from the Global South to embrace and articulate critical decolonial ethics of liberation as the foundation of a new politics of life as opposed to imperial politics of death. Previous decolonial humanists like Mahatma Gandhi, Aime Cesaire, William E.B. Du Bois, C.L.R. James, Albert Luthuli, Thomas Sankara, Frantz Fanon, Kenneth

Kaunda, and many others, were also opposed to the paradigm of war (Cesaire 1955; James 1963; Du Bois 1965; Fanon 1968; Falola 2001; Rabaka 2010). For decolonization and deimperialization were considered to be essential prerequisites for the paradigm of peace to prevail. It had to be followed by the return of humanism as a foundation of a socialist society where there was no exploitation of human beings by others.

This is why former president Kenneth Kaunda of Zambia, despite being criticized in some quarters for being a dictator who presided over a one-party state, is in other circles celebrated as one of the leading advocates of humanism, as indicated in the Mulugushi Declaration (Kaunda and Morris 1966). Others, like former president Leopold Sedar Senghor of Senegal, articulated humanism in terms of negritude and socialism. Notably, it was Senghor (1967) who described socialism as a form of humanism. It was also Senghor who explained that when he and Aime Cesaire formulated the term 'negritude' in the 1930s they were plunged into a state of panic and despair as the horizon of liberation was blocked, and colonialists were justifying colonialism using the theory of the *tabula rasa*. Negritude as a liberatory utopia emerged in struggle, as Africans struggled 'to divest ourselves of our borrowed attire – that of assimilation – and assert our being; that is to say our *negritude*' (Senghor, cited in Ahluwalia 2003: 32).

Just like Senghor, the former president of Tanzania Julius Nyerere understood humanism in terms of African socialism, which he tried to implement in the form of *Ujamaa villages* (Nyerere 1968). In like manner, Kwame Nkrumah, former president of Ghana, articulated humanism in terms of African personality, concienscism and pan-Africanism. Nkrumah (1964: 70) advocated for a new harmonious African society born out of a synthesis of Islamic, Euro-Christian and African values. Mandela understood humanism as *Ubuntu* as a foundation for a rainbow nation (Mandela 1994). Therefore here the concept of humanism is used to mean all those progressive efforts evolved by colonized and racialized subjects in the course of their struggle to regain their lost ontological density. This point was well captured by the

**47**

leading African novelist and humanist Chinua Achebe when he said:

> You have all heard of the African personality; of African democracy; of African way to socialism, of negritude, and so on. They are all props we have fashioned at different times to help us get on our feet again. Once we are up we shall not need any of them anymore. But for the moment it is in the nature of things that we may need to counter racism with what Jean-Paul Satre has called anti-racist racism, to announce not just that we are as good as the next man but that we are better. (Achebe, in Ahluwalia 2001: 61)

The paradigm of peace is therefore inextricably linked with decoloniality. It is made possible by 'decolonial turn'. Du Bois in 1903 announced decolonial turn as a rebellion against what he termed the 'colour line' that was constitutive of the core problems of the twentieth century. By the problem of the 'colour line', Du Bois was speaking of increasing racism and the forms of resistance and opposition that it was provoking. But broadly stated, a decolonial turn embodies critical decolonial ethics of liberation:

> It posits the primacy of ethics as an antidote to problems with Western conceptions of freedom, autonomy and equality, as well as the necessity of politics to forge a world where ethical relations become the norm rather than the exception. The de-colonial turn highlights the epistemic relevance of the enslaved and colonized search for humanity. (Maldonado-Torres 2008b: 7)

The leading African scholar and novelist Ngugi wa Thiong'o (1993, 2009) expressed the decolonial turn in terms of 'moving the centre' (from Eurocentrism/Europhonism to a plurality of cultures) towards 're-membering Africa' (addressing Africa's fragmentation that was imposed by imperialism and colonialism, and restoring African ontological density and cultural identity). Decolonial turn is rooted in struggles against racism, the slave trade, imperialism, colonialism and apartheid. But as noted by Maldonado-Torres (2008b: 7), the decolonial turn 'began to take definitive form after the end of the Second World War and the beginnings of the wars for liberation of many colonised countries soon after'.

# Critical Decolonial Ethics vs. Postcolonialism

A critical decolonial ethics of liberation differs from postcolonial approaches that became dominant in the 1990s in a number of ways. Genealogically, decoloniality and critical decolonial ethics of liberation are traceable to the anti-slave trade, anti-imperialist, anti-colonial and anti-apartheid thinkers originating from the Global South, whereas postcolonialism is traceable from thinkers from the Global North, such as Michel Foucault, Jacques Derrida, and Antonio Gramsci, among many others. Built on top of poststructuralism and postmodernism, postcolonialism was then popularized by those scholars from the Global South working in North American academies, such as Edward Said (1978), Homi Bhabha (1994), Gayatri Spivak (1994), Achille Mbembe (2001) and others.

While decoloniality begins its interventions from 1492 covering Spanish and Portuguese imperialism that was constitutive of the first phase of the rise of Eurocentric modernity, postcolonial interventions are focused on later British and to some extent French colonialism of the nineteenth century as their departure point. Decoloniality traces coloniality to the dawn of Euro-North American-centric modernity. Coloniality is in fact articulated in decoloniality as the underside of modernity. As such, modernity is unmasked by decoloniality whereas postcolonialism, because of its genealogical relationship with poststructuralism and postmodernism, is concerned with attacking meta-narratives and ideological certitudes. Decoloniality grapples with what Grosfoguel (2007) terms heterarchies of power, knowledge and being that sustain an asymmetrical world system and its imperial/colonial global orders.

In terms of horizon, decoloniality seeks to attain a decolonized and deimperialized world in which new pluriversal humanity is possible. Postcolonialism is part of a 'critique of modernity within modernity'. As such, postcolonialism becomes just another critical social theory cascading from the centre of the Euro-North American world just like liberalism, Marxism, poststructuralism and postmodernism. These critical social theoretical interventions

**49**

do not adequately address what decolonial theorists term coloniality as the underside/darker side of Euro-North American-centric modernity. Decoloniality gestures towards pluriversality (a world within which many worlds fit harmoniously and coexist peacefully). This is in tandem with Mandela's push for *ubuntu* (the African ethic of community, co-humanness, unity and harmony) and 'rainbow nation' (Campbell 2013). Chinweizu (2008) wrote of 'ubuntology', which he defined as the Afrocentric human sciences for black redemption that privileges African experience as its locus of enunciation.

## Mandela as an Embodiment of the Paradigm of Peace

A paradigm of peace is founded of humanism and justice. Mandela's life of struggle and his legacy is an embodiment of a consistent and active search for peace and harmony. In his autobiography, Mandela stated:

> I always know that deep down in every human heart, there [is] mercy and generosity. No one is born hating another person because of the colour of his skin, or his background, or his religion. People must learn to hate, and if they can learn to hate, they can be taught love, for love comes more naturally to the human heart than its opposite. Even the grimmest times in prison, when my comrades and I were pushed to our limits, I would see a glimmer of humanity in one of the guards, perhaps just for a second, but it was enough to assure me and keep me going. Man's goodness is a flame that can be hidden but never extinguished. (Mandela 1994: 609)

Mandela in a typical decolonial ethics of liberation interpreted the anti-colonial/anti-apartheid struggle as a humanistic movement for restoration of human life. This is how he put it: 'This then is what the ANC is fighting for. Their struggle is a truly national one. It is a struggle of the African people, inspired by their own suffering and their own experience. *It is a struggle for the right to live* (my emphasis) (ibid.: 352). This paradigm of peace marks a radical humanistic-oriented departure from the paradigm of war. It is premised on a radically humanistic phenomenology of liberation aimed at rescuing those people reduced by racism to the category of the 'wretched of the earth' through recovery of their lost ontological density, epistemic virtues, and agency. Thus what one gleans from Mandela's *Long Walk to Freedom* is that, in the face of apartheid officials and institutionalized racism as well as brutality and intolerance of dissent, he emerged as the advocate of decolonization, a fighter for freedom, and the face of new non-racial inclusive humanism.

It would also seem that Mandela was ahead of his time. This is evident from his clear articulation of the discourse of democracy and human rights long before it became a major global normative issue for many other political actors and leaders at the end of the Cold War. But Mandela had already vowed to die for democracy and free society as far back as the 1960s.

What is also distinctive about Mandela is that he did not easily dismiss the Euro-North American modernist project of emancipation. He fought for the realization of those positive aspects of it that were denied to Africans but were enjoyed in Europe and North America. Here was an African located in the 'zone of non-being' (Fanon 1968) claiming entitlement to the fruits of Euro-North American-centric modernity on the basis of being a human being with equal ontological density to those residing in Europe and the white colonialists resident in Africa. In this way Mandela was directly challenging the Euro-North American-centric global order founded on racism. During this time, some leading African freedom fighters like Julius Nyerere (1968) were speaking of such other ideologies as African socialism and African forms of democracy as more authentic projects for the continent.

Mandela just pushed for democracy and human rights without putting 'African' as the adjective. This is why Slavoj Zizek (2013) has credited Mandela for providing a model of how to liberate a country from apartheid colonialism 'without succumbing to the temptation of dictatorial power and anti-capitalist posturing'. He elaborated that 'Mandela was not Mugabe' as he maintained South Africa as a multi-party democracy, ensuring that the vibrancy of the national economy was insulated from 'hasty socialist experiments' (ibid.). Mandela was worried more about denial of democracy rather than its Euro-North American genealogy and articulation. It seemed to Mandela that democracy and freedom were simple positive human values that have to be enjoyed by every human being, irrespective of race and location.

Interestingly, in his autobiography, Mandela also credited his Xhosa traditional society's mode of governance, which he described as 'democracy in its purest form' where everyone irrespective of societal rank was allowed space to 'voice their opinions and were [*sic*] equal in their value as citizens' (Mandela 1994: 20). At the same time, Mandela described himself as 'being something of an Anglophile', and confessed that '[w]hile I abhorred the notion of British imperialism, I never rejected the trappings of British style and manners' (ibid.: 48). Mandela always admired British parliamentary democracy. This became evident when he said:

> From the reading of Marxist literature and from conversations with Marxists, I have gained the impression that communists regard the parliamentary system of the West as undemocratic and reactionary. But, on the contrary, I am an admirer of such a system.
>
> The Magna Carta, the Petition of Rights and the Bill of Rights are documents which are held in veneration by democrats throughout the world. I have great respect for British political institutions, and for the country's system of justice. I regard the British Parliament as the most democratic institution in the world, and the independence and impartiality of its judiciary never fail to arouse my admiration. The American Congress, the country's doctrine of separation of powers, as well as the independence of its judiciary, arouse in me similar sentiments. (ibid.: 351)

The important point is that democracy must not be understood as an artefact or invention of Europeans. Europeans only appropriated it just like all other positive products of human history. Following this logic, Mandela was correct not to reject democracy. But he did not need to be an 'Anglophile' to claim democracy as a human value. Anyway, the English denied democracy to African people for centuries until Mandela and other African decolonial humanists fought for liberation, freedom and democracy.

## Mandela Phenomenon as a Synthesis of Various Ideologies

Raymond Suttner (2007: 119) warns us about trying 'to fit him into a specific political orientation'. He emphasizes that 'Mandela made his statements as a leader of a liberation movement trying to rally support from all quarters, especially those that had been hostile or indifferent to the struggle of the ANC. It was part of his mission to win them over to support the organization' (ibid.: 121). But it was Tom Lodge in his *Mandela: A Critical Life* (2006) who tried to specify Mandela's ideological orientation based on the statements he made. He even argued that Mandela embraced liberal ideas. Suttner (2007) challenged such a reading of Mandela, arguing that when Mandela spoke he did not do so as an individual expressing his own political ideological orientation and preferences. Instead, Mandela spoke as a leader of a movement that was involved in mobilizing the world to its own side:

> Mandela's court statements addressed the world as a national leader. Mandela did not speak as a 'dissident', that is, a representative of a minority view, but projected a national vision to the people of South Africa and the world at large. As indicated, such self-representation required an attempt to reach many audiences and could not be sectarian or limited in its appeal. (Suttner 2007: 121)

Other scholars like Stephen Ellis in *Comrades Against Apartheid: The ANC and the South African Communist Party in Exile* (1992, with T. Sechaba) and in *External Mission: The ANC in Exile* (2013) tried to highlight that Mandela was a communist. Ellis elaborated: 'The revelation that Mandela was a prominent Communist Party member does not distract from his historic stature. It does, however, mean that the version of history propagated by the ANC, which [has] governed South Africa since 1994, is seriously flawed' (Ellis 2011: 1). To buttress his argument that Mandela was a communist, Ellis quoted Joe Slovo, a leading member of SACP, who said: 'We sent Nelson off to Africa a communist, and he came back an African Nationalist (Ellis 2013: 33). Perhaps Slovo did not understand Mandela's deep nationalist decolonial humanist political orientation. Garth le Pere, in an elongated review of Ellis's book *The External Mission: The ANC in Exile,* correctly noted that 'Mandela's real or imagined SACP membership is really much ado about nothing by Ellis' (le Pere 2014: 4). If one reads Ellis's book closely it is dominated by a frantic attempt to discredit the ANC and to project the SACP as the dominant political force that spearheaded the liberation struggle in exile, while at the same time appropriating Mandela as a communist. But Ellis fails to sustain the argument, particularly with regards to how the ANC emerged as the leading voice during the CODESA negotiations if it was indeed playing second fiddle to the SACP during the course of the liberation struggle. Worse still, Ellis seems to take the SACP position uncritically in a struggle in which liberation forces were in competition for dominance and leadership.

The question of whether Mandela was a communist or not, is indeed 'much ado about nothing by Ellis' as advanced by le Pere. It adds nothing to a deeper understanding of the Mandela phenomenon except to reveal that Mandela, like all other anti-colonial/decolonial humanists, was open to various ideological resources as long as they had a potential to enrich the people's struggle for liberation. Ellis's intention is revealed when he writes that 'the ANC in power has remained little interested in understanding the world as it is or has become', and also when he argues that 'the ANC has blithely continued since 1994 to suppose that the rest of the world still has special regard for the ANC as the bearer of the moral torch' (Ellis 2013: 300–4). If these two arguments are closely examined, one cannot avoid reaching a conclusion that Ellis's project has been one of doing everything to discredit the ANC as a liberation movement, including robbing it of Mandela's membership. Le Pere provides a convincing rebuttal to this take on the ANC:

This is an astounding assertion for a party that can justifiably claim a progressive foreign policy that has positioned South Africa in the epicenter of world politics and international relations ... The ANC under the presidencies of Mandela and Mbeki enjoyed strong international support because the ANC had an unassailable moral claim to govern by virtue of its growing international legitimacy and its subsequent electoral victories. The strength of this moral currency has only recently depreciated with the poor administration, rising levels of corruption and misrule under President Jacob Zuma. (Le Pere 2014: 5)

Mandela's views on communism are detailed in his autobiography and conversations with himself. He revealed that he read Marxist literature, attended Communist Party meetings, questioned communism as a foreign ideology and still attended night schools on communism. There is abundant evidence of how the ANC and SACP worked closely with each other throughout the liberation struggle. Ellis's intervention on this issue is another attempt to ideologically tag Mandela at any cost. On Robben Island, Mandela even taught a course on political economy that was informed by Marxist thought (Mandela 1994: 455). It is also public knowledge that Mandela met Moses Kotane (by then Secretary General of the South African Communist Party) every night before the Rivonia Trials (Suttner 2003: 134–35).

The point is that there is no doubt that Mandela like many African leaders was influenced by many ideological currents ranging from African tradition to Christianity, liberalism and communism. Whether this must lead scholars to try and pin down such leaders as Mandela to a particular ideology is another matter. Depicting Mandela as a decolonial humanist par excellence might partly solve the problem of his ideological orientation because decolonial humanism is constituted by a family of ideologies that privilege 'being' as the main issue.

What must be emphasized is that Mandela's political thought and ideological orientation was forged in the crucible of racial oppression, at the centre of which were complex questions of defining 'the people', the nation, belonging, political community, citizenship and ideology. Mandela was an active actor resisting the narrow and exclusivist racial definition and articulation of all these questions as well as an active builder of a broader inclusive South African nationalism. C.R.D. Halisi (1999) identified two dominant ideological strands that dominated the South African decolonial-nationalist struggle. The first was what he termed 'racial nationalism', which 'persisted as a potent political force throughout the colonial, postcolonial and apartheid eras of racial domination' (ibid.: 1). The second was the multiracial nationalism that gestured towards a multiracial nation within a singular, unitary, democratic and post-apartheid state.

According to Halisi, black racial nationalism just like white racial nationalism portended a particular conception of citizenship. This form of citizenship took the form of republican exclusivist orientation. Multiracial nationalism gestured towards liberal inclusive citizenship. He identified this as 'a core antinomy of black thought for Africans'. He elaborated:

> In a very fundamental sense, the struggle for liberation required black activists to confront nascent questions of citizenship and national identity – how the 'people' are to be defined, who belongs to the political community, and what are the criteria of inclusion and exclusion. In brief, differences between multiracialists and black nationalists over the social character of the liberation struggle were often predicated on rival conceptions of citizenship. (Halisi 1999: 4)

Understanding these complex issues enables us to gain a deeper understanding of the socio-political milieu within which Mandela's ideological formation emerged. The tension between race-consciousness and non-racial perspectives emerged as political actors tried to interpret black condition and map the contours of black liberation. The catalytic debates were 'over the meanings of liberation, democracy and, by extension, citizenship' (ibid.: 7). By the 1970s, the Marxist class struggle oriented discourse of liberation complicated the ideological debates even further, as did the rise of black consciousness discourse of liberation. It is clear from his biography that Mandela's political and ideological orientation shifted from a radical Africanism of the 1940s that was suspicious of the inclusion of whites and Indians in the African liberation struggle, to the Charterist ideology of the 1950s. What emerged poignantly was an ANC–SACP nationalist-liberal-Marxism that was gesturing towards a non-racial post-apartheid nation. This hybrid brand of revolutionary thought sought to accommodate the topical race–class controversy.

On the other hand, there was a strong Africanism which had foundations in a radical Africanist reading of the South African situation. The Africanist reading of South African history of oppression, exploitation and domination emphasized that European settlers had dispossessed Africans of their ancestral lands, in the process making the African people constitute a homogenous community of dispossessed people that had to fight for liberation as a cohesive force. This cohesive force must operate as an intra-racial multi-class alliance (Halisi 1999: 62). The liberation of workers was a subset of the broader liberation of the black nation from domination by a white nation. What was needed for both race-conscious nationalism and non-racial nationalism was the ability to stretched and indigenized Marxist revolutionary theory to reflect the African reality. This is why Halisi (ibid.: 63) writes of 'reconstructed versions of Marxism resulting in a melding of anti-colonial, anti-capitalist and anti-racist ideologies'.

Mandela was ideologically caught up in the alchemy of South African struggle, with its ability not only to transcend the legacy of bifurcated citizenship but also to carefully synthesize various ideological traditions ranging from liberalism to Marxism, Africanism, ethnic republicanism, black consciousness and pan-Africanism. This point is very important for one to gain a deeper understanding of Mandela, whose ideological orientation was constituted by a synthesis and a compromise of all usable floating political resources for a decolonial humanist struggle for a post-racial society. The long-standing challenge, however, is well captured by Halisi when he writes that:

> Rival populisms, nourished by the competing visions of liberation, are bound to have an impact on the evolution of South African citizenship. In addition, popular democratic traditions, of which populism is one manifestation, are among the most durable sources of inspiration for democratic thinkers. After centuries of racial domination, it would be unrealistic to expect an ethos of nonracial citizenship to prevail unchallenged by older political perceptions. Eventually, the black liberation struggle may come to be viewed by all South Africans as a national achievement and, therefore, a cornerstone of nonracial citizenship identity. For the immediate

The Decolonial Mandela

future, however, successive governments will have to cope with the implications of both nonracial and race-conscious political sensibilities. (Halisi 1999: 133)

The Mandela phenomenon existed as an attempt to bridge the long-standing liberal–republican dichotomy. This attempt raised the next challenge for a moderate Mandela who lived to mediated forces of separation versus integration, racial consciousness versus non-racialism, as well as black power versus civil rights. This challenge is linked to that of his ideological orientation. As noted by Alexander Beresford (2014: 1), 'One dominant narrative that emerged in tributes to Mandela was his famed capacity to moderate between competing social forces during the transition'. This characterization of Mandela was reinforced by those who credited Mandela with preventing a full-scale racial war in South Africa. For example, Richard Stengel (2009: 121) depicted Mandela as that politician that 'always saw both sides of every issue, and his default position was to find some course in between, some way of reconciling both sides'. Does this make Mandela a moderate? Beresford (2014: 2) defined moderates as people who 'occupy the ideological centre ground or "soft-end" of a political extreme, reconcile competing political views or ideological standpoints, and/or defend and maintain the political and economic status quo'.

Mandela did not struggle to 'defend and maintain the political and economic status quo' of apartheid. But at the same time he worked hard to moderate extreme political standpoints. Mandela was not ideologically neutral. He was a nationalist-liberal-decolonial humanist who also embraced positive African qualities and values cascading from precolonial times. As far as the economy is concerned, Mandela initially embraced the ideology of nationalization of the commanding heights of the economy but later, after his release from prison, he favoured 'a mixed economy approach with a heavy presence of the state in crucial economic sectors' (Beresford 2014: 4; see also Peet 2002: 71). Mandela had this to say about his approach to politics and leadership:

The masses like to see someone who is responsible and who speaks to them in a responsible manner. They like that, and I want to avoid rabble-rousing speech. I don't want to incite the crowd. I want the crowd to understand what we are doing and I want to infuse a spirit of reconciliation ... I have mellowed, very definitely, and as a young man, you know, I was very radical and using high-flown language, and fighting everybody. But now, you know, one has to lead. (Mandela 2010: 54)

Mandela was not so much a moderate as a pragmatist. This pragmatism even explains his approach to the use of violence in a liberation struggle. In the face of the full wrath and violence of the notorious apartheid system that directly threatened to cut short his own life through charging him for treason, Mandela maintained a steadfast commitment to decolonial ethics of liberation, and refused to compromise on his humanist principles. He lamented how the apartheid system was leaving him with no option but to engage in counter-violence as form of defence for those fighting against apartheid. Does Mandela fit into the mould of Mahatma Gandhi or Martin Luther King, who strongly believed in non-violent civil disobedience?

Suttner (2007: 120) outrightly dismisses the applicability of Gandhism to Mandela: 'Clearly in the case of Mandela, the notion of Gandhism is quite inapplicable'. Mandela was instrumental in the formation of 'uMkonto We Sizwe' (Spear of the Nation) and became its commander-in-chief. This was the armed wing of the African National Congress. The MK fighting forces were expected to adhere to strict ethical conduct of only engaging in destabilization and not in killing people. Even when Mandela was being tried for treason, he continued to tower above the apartheid system's provocations, brutality and violence, and was able to invite the architects of apartheid to return to humanity in a moving speech delivered during the course of the Rivonia Trials:

> During my lifetime, I have dedicated myself to this struggle of the African people. I have fought against white domination, and I have fought against black domination. I have cherished the ideal of a democratic and free society in which all persons live together in harmony with equal opportunities. It is an ideal which I hope to live for and to see realized. But if needs be, it is an ideal for which I am prepared to die. (Mandela 1994: 352)

## Mandela and the Question of Violent Struggle

Mandela made it clear that the continued use of brutality and violence by the apartheid regime against unarmed anti-apartheid freedom fighters left them with no choice but 'to hit back by all means in our power in defence of our people, our future and our freedom' (Mandela 1994: 78). The historical record indicates that there were long debates within the ANC over the question of adoption of the armed struggle, and Mandela and many others participated actively in these debates. What has often been ignored in these debates is that various forms of violent resistance were underway in such places as Zeerust, Sekhukhuneland, Mpondoland, Natal and Zululand that assumed the form of popular rural insurrections, and indicated the preparedness of a colonized people to fight for life within a killing apartheid colonial context (Magubane et al. 2004: 52–59). The consequence of these developments was that 'the ANC in the 1950s and early 1960s found itself facing demands not only for political support, but also military assistance. First the Sekhukhuneland rebels and then their Mpondo counterparts asked the ANC leadership for guns so that they could pursue their goals more effectively' (ibid.: 53–54). It would seem that events on the ground were moving too fast for the ANC leadership to embrace anti-colonial violence as a redemptive option. Mandela played a leading role in motivating for a shift from non-violent resistance to violent resistance. Was Mandela therefore thinking and acting like a Fanonian who appreciated redemptive qualities of anti-colonial violence? Suttner (2007: 120) argued that '[f]or Mandela there was a clear preference for non-violence, as is the case with most revolutionaries'. But he elaborated that 'the question whether or not one can continue to pursue non-violence is not decided in the first place by those who experience oppressive rule. Whether or not one can continue to pursue a non-violent path and achieve political goals is determined by the character and extent of the space allowed for legal public activity' (ibid.).

The ANC maintained throughout the anti-apartheid struggle that it adopted violence and the armed struggle as a last resort.

Mandela's ideas on violence might therefore fit into the Fanonian notions of anti-colonial violence, which is often misunderstood to mean that Fanon was an advocate of violence as the only solution to the colonizer–colonized problem. Fanon distinguished between colonial violence and anti-colonial violence, in that the latter is not 'ideological' but 'is the absolute opposite of colonial violence' (Mbembe 2013: 14; Fanon 1968). Achille Mbembe puts the logic of Fanonian anti-colonial violence more clearly when he says: 'It takes the form of pure discharge – ad hoc violence, reptilian and convulsive, a deadly gesture and elemental affect that results in the "hunted man", "back to the wall", "knife to his throat" or, to be more specific, confusedly to "show he is poised to fight for his life"' (Mbembe 2013: 14).

Anti-colonial violence must therefore be understood as part of a human instinct for self-preservation. It is informed by the will to live. It is meant to produce life and new humanism. As Mbembe (ibid.) puts it: 'The Fanonian theory of violence has no meaning without a greater framework, that of the ascent towards humanity'. It is a violence discharged by those people who have been pushed by coloniality against the hall – a people fighting for life itself. But Jonathan Hyslop dismissed the identity of Mandela as a Fanonian:

> In recent years, an antithetical view has arisen among some writers in the tradition of postcolonial theory: a conception of Mandela as an anti-colonial revolutionary in the lineage of Frantz Fanon, favouring the purifying violence of insurrection by the oppressed. And in some cases, he is portrayed as oscillating between a violent Fanonism and a peaceful Gandhianism. But Mandela was no Fanonian either. Unlike the revolutionary psychoanalysts, he never thought of armed resistance as offering any healing power for the colonized. Mandela's ideas about the use of force were pragmatic and instrumental. He was, indeed, influenced by leaders of the anti-colonial movement in which Fanon participated, the Algerian National Liberation Front (FLN). But their advice pointed him in a very different direction from that suggested by Fanon's theories. And Mandela's ethical approach to the use of force was informed by exactly the kind of humanist ideas that Fanon and postcolonial theorists eschew. (Hyslop 2014: 163)

Just like in his ability to draw inspiration from different ideological springs in his advancement of the anti-colonial struggle, Mandela was also open to different military doctrines. He read Tolstoy's *War and Peace* as well as Clausewitz's magnum opus *On War*, while at the same time expressing a deep appreciation of precolonial African leaders like King Shaka of the Zulu's tactics and strategies. He made it clear that he read military literature as part of his search for principles of starting an armed revolution (Mandela 2010: 53). Hyslop (2014: 162–65) prefers to label Mandela as 'Clausewitzian' and a pragmatic 'Nehruist' rather than a 'utopian Gandhi' or a 'violent Fanon'. But Mandela also said: 'Heroes like the Khoi leader [Autshumayo], Maqoma of the Rharhabe, Bambatha, Cetshwayo of the Zulu, Mampuru of the Pedis, Tshivashe of the Vendas and a host of others were in the forefront of wars of resistance, and we speak of them with respect and admiration' (Mandela 2010: 31). This historical knowledge proved that Mandela read widely about African primary resistance too. So it is difficult to assign him a catch-all label like 'Clausewitzian', just like it is difficult to pigeonhole him into one ideological strand such as liberalism. To label him a decolonial humanist is more appropriate because it is open ended. Mandela's preparedness to die for a democratic and free society cast him more as a 'radical' African humanist who fully embraced the ideals of ethics, democracy, equality, freedom, and human rights. Colonial powers denied Africans these values. For Africa, these values were part of the rhetoric of Euro-American-centric modernity and were never extended to black people (Ndlovu-Gatsheni 2013c). These values were only practised in Europe and North America.

As noted by Maldonado-Torres (2007, 2008b) and other decolonial theorists, ethics were suspended when it came to dealing with Africans who inhabited what Fanon termed the 'zone of non-being' (Fanon 1968). Should those fighting against colonialism and its legacy also suspend ethics? Should white settler colonial conquest be re-conquered violently for Africans to realize social and economic justice? How should those fighting for decolonial civilization deal with unrepentant racists? These are some of the difficult questions that haunt the Mandela phenomenon. Should those who denied 'being' itself to Africans, who wrote them out of the nation and excluded them from citizenship, be made to test their medicine as has been the case in Zimbabwe? Perhaps a useful way to deal with these questions is to compare and contrast the approaches used by Mandela and Robert Gabriel Mugabe to deal with complex native and settler questions in South Africa and Zimbabwe respectively. Mugabe is not chosen randomly here. He is another leading African leader who has been caught up in controversial politics because of his continued anti-colonial and anti-imperialist position that has seen him leading his Zimbabwean people in new struggle for economic freedom in the twenty-first century.

## What Set Mandela Apart from Mugabe?

Mandela and Mugabe are both leading African national-ists. They both sacrificed a lot for those people who inhab-ited the 'zones of non-being'. They both pursued a policy of reconciliation. But Mugabe's 'policy' of reconciliation was never written down. It was pronounced as part of his Independence Speech in April 1980. Mugabe repudiated the 'policy' of reconciliation in 1997. The reason given for repudiation was that the whites minority Zimbabweans had refused to embrace reconciliation. The repudiation came at a time when Zimbabwe was preparing for a compulsory redistribution of land without compensation. Before Mugabe and Mandela, President Jomo Kenyatta of Kenya and President Julius Nyerere of Tanzania pursued the policies of reconciliation. Before Mandela was released from prison in 1990, Mugabe was the dominant leader in Southern Africa and a respected statesman in many parts of the world. Mugabe had spent ten years in prison and had also led the armed guerrilla liberation struggle for fifteen years. He became the first black leader of Zimbabwe in 1980. Just like Mandela, Mugabe had pronounced a policy of reconciliation in 1980, and also emphasized national unity, as leitmotifs of his nation-building and state-making processes (Ndlovu-Gatsheni 2009a). But the policy of reconciliation, despite being proclaimed from

**63**

a high moral ground, might fundamentally reproduce coloniality, particularly in a context where negotiations tended to be in defence of the colonial status quo. The Lancaster House negotiations involved Western superpowers who were intent on protecting white minority rights.

The Patriotic Front of Mugabe and Joshua Nkomo did not push hard enough for a genuine decolonial outcome in which it was possible to destroy the colonial economic power structures that privileges white settlers over black indigenous people of Zimbabwe. The fundamental question for both Mugabe and Mandela was about their approach towards becoming decolonial humanists. For Zimbabwe, it is clear that the policy of reconciliation was somehow imposed on Mugabe, hence it remained just a proclamation and was never written into any substantive national policy. But what became even more worrying in Mugabe's postcolonial governance practice was the reproduction of colonial violence in dealing with those excluded from the nation. For example, his emphasis on national unity was compromised by the way he deployed a highly partisan army into Matebeleland and Midlands regions, which then committed horrendous atrocities, killing over twenty thousand Ndebele-speaking people (Catholic Commission for Justice and Peace and Legal Resources Foundation Report 1997). The pretext for this was that there were dissidents operating in Matebeleland and the Midlands regions who sought to destabilize the country.

However, the signing of the Unity Accord on 22 December 1987 that resulted in the ending of Fifth Brigade atrocities in Matebeleland and the Midlands regions boosted Mugabe's stature as a statesman and a nation builder who managed to unite his people and brought to an end a low-intensity civil war without external intervention. The reality, however, is that the statesman was not Mugabe but Joshua Nkomo who withstood extreme provocations and direct threats to his own life and spoke the language of national unity during a time when Mugabe and his government were speaking of eradicating the entire Ndebele-speaking population and were entertaining tribalization of the nation from above.

It would seem that Mugabe's leadership of a protracted armed guerrilla struggle led him to embrace the paradigm of war as a solution to intractable political questions. His ideology of *Chimurenga* articulated the history of Zimbabwe as dominated by a series of armed nationalist revolutions from 1896 right up to his widely condemned *Third Chimurenga* of the 2000s (Ndlovu-Gatsheni 2012b). Because of Mugabe's embrace of the paradigm of war, governance in Zimbabwe has been dominated by what Martin Rupiya (2005) termed 'governance by military operations'. His celebration of the *Third Chimurenga*, particularly the Fast Track Land Reform Programme facet of it, in terms of prevailing sovereignty of Zimbabwean nationalism over settler colonialism as well as triumph of conquest of conquest, support the idea of Mugabe as a Nietzschean thinker who fully embraced the paradigm of war. This is how he put it: 'We are now talking of conquest of conquest, the prevailing sovereignty of the people of Zimbabwe over settler minority rule and all it stood for including the possession of our land ... Power to the people must now be followed by land to the people' (The *Herald*, 6 December 1997). Consequently, in Zimbabwe the paradigm of war is celebrated in music to the extent that those in ZANU-PF, including Mugabe, have openly told the nation that they have a proud history in violence and they have earned 'degrees in violence' (Blair 2002). The degrees in violence gained as Zimbabwean African nationalists were forced to confront white colonial violence with nationalist violence.

Besides this, a toxic, xenophobic and racist national discourse has been promoted as a necessary ideological resource in the struggle to complete the unfinished decolonization project and reverse the legacy of white settler colonialism. The consequences have, on the one hand, been the alienation of the Ndebele-speaking community from the nation and the disfranchisement of white commercial farmers, and on the other hand, a 'successful' land reform and ongoing indigenization of the national economy drive (Muzondidya 2010). Mugabe has lamented that his policy of reconciliation has never been reciprocated by the minority whites who continued to own large tracks of land and were never prepared to share it with the indigenous black people. Is Mugabe wrong to use the paradigm of war to take the decolonization project to the realm of economic independence? Is there another option? These are difficult questions to answer. But the land-hungry peasants have welcomed Mugabe's solution as pragmatic. Mugabe himself has criticized Mandela's solution as informed by saintly discourse that made him fail to confront and transform white economic power in South Africa. Mugabe is very popular among the unemployed youth and land-hungry South Africans. Mugabe always receives a hero's welcome when he visits South Africa. Perhaps this popular support for Mugabe reflects the limits of Mandela's approach?

Mandela's liberation struggle was also aimed at the liberation of both the oppressed and the oppressors from the cul-de-sac of racialism in the truly Freireian resolution of the oppressor–oppressed contradiction created by colonialism and coloniality (Freire 1970). On this Mandela wrote:

> It was during those long and lonely years that my hunger for the freedom of my people became a hunger for the freedom of all people, white and black. I knew as well as I know anything that the oppressor must be liberated just as surely as the oppressed. A man who takes away another man's freedom is a prisoner of hatred; he is locked behind the bars of prejudice and narrow-mindedness. I am not truly free if I am taking away someone else's freedom, just as surely as I am not free when my freedom is taken from me. The oppressed and the oppressor alike are robbed of their humanity. (Mandela 1994: 611)

This set him apart from Mugabe who ended up frustrated by the policy of reconciliation and finally reproduced the colonial paradigm of war of conquest predicated on race. By the end of 1990s, President Mugabe increasingly articulated the decolonial project in Zimbabwe in racist, nativist and even xenophobic terms predicated on the idea of 'conquest of conquest', 'prevailing sovereignty of Zimbabwe over settler colonialism, and the notion of 'Zimbabwe for Zimbabweans' (Ndlovu-Gatsheni 2009a, 2009b). Perhaps if Mandela had been young when he took over the reins of power and if he had served long presidential terms as Mugabe, maybe he also would have been frustrated by a lack of transformative movement, and revoked the policy of reconciliation? But he only served one presidential term and voluntarily retired from active politics, making it somewhat unfair to compare and contrast him with Mugabe who has been in power for over three decades. But one cannot escape commenting that unlike Mandela's nationalism, Mugabe's nationalism had escalated to what appeared like 'reverse racism' as a form of liberation as he pushed for a fast-track land reform programme predicated on compulsory land acquisition from white commercial farmers to give it to black Zimbabweans (Mugabe 2001). Mugabe justified his actions in this way: 'This country is our country and this land is our land … They think because are white they have a divine right to our resources. Not here. The white man is not indigenous to Africa. Africa is for Africans. Zimbabwe is for Zimbabweans' (Quoted in Ndlovu-Gatsheni 2009a: 67). Unlike Mandela, Mugabe was openly articulating that land reform discourse in a somewhat reverse-black-racism. But despite the racist sentiments in Mugabe's justifications of his land reform programme, that he committed himself to making sure that land was fairly distributed to the landless Zimbabweans was a progressive decolonial idea. Such a move is part of furthering decoloniality. What became open to intense debates were the methods used. But no one has offered an alternative methodology of dealing with the emotive land question. The discourse of 'willing-buyer' and 'willing-seller' seems not to be effective. A large constituency of black people never expected to buy the land that they consider to have been stolen from their ancestors by white colonialists. This is why James Muzondidya argued that:

> Far from being exhausted, the political rhetoric on race, black economic empowerment and radical, exclusive black nationalism, despite all the ambiguities and contradictions, continued to resonate with many Zimbabweans in both rural and urban areas who recognized the unfair balance of ownership of land and other important economic resources between blacks and whites. (Muzondidya 2010: 13)

But the overt use of reverse-racial language rather than ethical decolonial humanist discourse that is free from racism nearly spoiled a progressive land reform programme in Zimbabwe. Fanon (1968) had warned of the dangers of degeneration of African nationalism into chauvinism, reverse racism, and xenophobia. He characterized this regressive process as 'repetition without change' cascading from pitfalls of national consciousness (Fanon 1968). It would seem Mandela carefully managed to distinguish himself as committed decolonial ethical leader and successfully avoided degeneration into reverse racism, nativism and xenophobia until his death, but at what cost to the decolonial transformation agenda remains a difficult question to answer.

## Mandela on the Question of Being Free

Mandela articulated the struggle for freedom as a 'long walk'. The concept of a 'long walk' captures how the struggle involved expenditure of human energy. In the concept of a 'long walk' there is the element of sacrifice and commitment towards reaching a certain destination. To Mandela the 'long walk' included 'walking through the shadow of death' in search of freedom. It would seem from the allegory of the struggle of freedom as a 'long walk', Mandela understood freedom as a form of 'arrival'. Indeed since the dawn of Euro-North American-centric modernity and the colonial encounters, black people have been walking a 'long walk' to freedom. Such events and processes as the slave trade, imperialism, partition, colonialism and apartheid constituted the 'shadows of death'. Prosecution and imprisonment of those who decided to lead in this 'long walk' directly threatened life of the African leaders.

But Mandela also meditated deeply and critically on the question of being free. This is what he wrote:

*I was not born with a hunger to be free. I was born free – free in every way that I could know.* Free to run in the fields near my mother's hut, free to swim in the clear stream that ran through my village, free to roast mealies under the stars and ride the broad backs of slow-moving bulls. As long as I obeyed my father and abided by the customs of my tribe, I was not troubled by the laws of man or God.

It was only when I began to learn that my boyhood freedom was an illusion, when I discovered as a young man that my freedom had already been taken from me, that I began to hunger for it … It was this desire for the freedom of my people to live their lives with dignity and self-respect that animated my life, that transformed a frightened young man into a bold one, that drove a law-abiding attorney to become a criminal, that turned a family-loving husband into a man without a home, that forced a life-loving man to live like a monk. (Mandela 1994: 610; my emphasis)

Mandela's meditation on freedom – which he enjoyed in childhood but later realized was nominal, even false and illusionary – is illuminating on the black experience. It remind us that men and women were indeed all born equal but they did not remain equal the rest of their lives because of historical circumstances of patriarchy, colonialism and coloniality (Tlostanova and Mignolo 2012: 155). This take on freedom speaks to the fundamental question of who is the 'human' that is evoked in the human rights discourse.

The question of who is the 'human' in the global human rights discourse is a pertinent one in a world where people from the (ex)-colonized world had to fight to be accepted as human beings. It invites decolonial thinkers and theorists to delve deeper into the histories of 'losing equality since the origins of the world' (Tlostanova and Mignolo 2012: 155). The slave trade might be the best beginning on this history in which black people began to lose their ontological density, equality and rights.

This approach might inaugurate another discourse of human rights cascading from those parts of the world inhabited by people who experienced denial of their humanity, who Tlostanova and Mignolo (ibid.: 164) have depicted as 'the *anthropos* of the planet' as opposed to the 'humitas'. What Mandela was fighting against is a system of power that transformed black people who were born free into 'anthropos of the planet'. But Mandela has been clear on the deeper meaning of what it entails to be free – it involves regaining lost ontological density (human dignity and self-respect) and agency (ability to decide and shape one's life). This struggle is not yet won. Mandela was also clear that 1994 was not a moment of 'arrival'. This is clear from the concluding paragraphs of his *Long Walk to Freedom*:

> When I walked out of prison, that was my mission, to liberate the oppressed and the oppressor both. Some say that has now been achieved. But I know that is not the case. The truth is that we are not yet free; we have merely achieved the freedom to be free, the right not to be oppressed. We have not taken the final step of our journey, but the first step on a longer and even more difficult road. For to be free is not merely to cast off one's chains, but to live in a way that respects and enhances the freedom of others. The true test of our devotion to freedom is just beginning.
>
> I have walked that long road to freedom. I have tried not to falter; I have made missteps along the way. But have discovered the secret that after climbing a great hill, one finds that there are many more hills to climb. I have taken a moment here to rest, to steal a view of the glorious vista that surrounds me, to look back on the distance I have come. But I can rest only for a moment, for with freedom comes responsibility, and I dare not linger, for my long walk is not yet ended. (Mandela 1994: 611)

Indeed the African decolonial struggle is still on course mainly because the post-1945 decolonization project failed to deliver a genuinely decolonized and deimperialized world. The idea of a decolonized post-1945 world that was defined in simplistic terms of elimination of direct colonial administrations and their replacement with African-led government amounted to what Grosfoguel depicted as 'the most powerful myths of the twentieth century'. No postcolonial world was born because:

> The heterogeneous and multiple global structures put in place over a period of 450 years did not evaporate with the juridical-political decolonization of the periphery over the past 50 years. We continue to live under the same 'colonial power matrix'. With juridical-political decolonization we moved from a period of 'global colonialism' to the current period of 'global coloniality'. (Grosfoguel 2007: 219)

Mandela was fully aware of this. This is why he concluded his autobiography by saying 'for my long walk is not yet ended'.

# Two

# Mandela
## Different Lives in One

## Introduction

> Of course you cannot know a man completely, his character, his
> principles, sense of judgment, not till he's shown his colours, ruling
> people, making laws.
>
> Experience, there is the test.
> – Play *Antigone*, cited in Mandela, *Long Walk to Freedom*

> Most men, you know, are influenced by their background. I grew
> up in a country village ... going to school for the greater part of the
> year, come back during the June and December holidays ... And
> then in 1941 when I was twenty-three, I came to Johannesburg and
> learned ... to absorb Western standards of living and so on. But
> ... my opinions were already formed from the countryside and ...
> you'll therefore appreciate my enormous respect for my culture ...
> Of course Western culture is something we cannot live without, so I
> have got these two strands of cultural influence
> – Mandela, *Conversations With Myself*

Nelson Rolihlahla Mandela's personal odyssey is from a young
Thembu/Xhosa/African boy born into a royal Thembu family in
Eastern Cape to a college-aged black activist, to a black nationalist based in Johannesburg exposed to various floating ideological streams and strands, to a founder of the ANC's military wing

known as Mkhonto we Sizwe (MK), to a prisoner of conscience, to a pragmatic advocate of nationalist-multiracial democracy, and finally to a world-renowned apostle of racial reconciliation and inclusive non-racial citizenship. This personal odyssey is also part of a macrocosm of the broader life struggle of many black South Africans. But to gain a deeper insight into the political formation of Mandela and the antinomies that shaped and even haunted his life, it is important to understand how it unfolded from childhood, because early experiences had an influence on his later views in maturity. It is often very difficult for human beings to step outside themselves successfully. Mandela is not an exception. Tom Lodge in *Mandela: A Critical Life* (2006) emphasized the importance of understanding Mandela's childhood:

How is my treatment of Mandela's life different from theirs? It is different in several ways. First of all, my understanding of Mandela's childhood and youth is, I think, more complicated than in the other narratives about his beginnings. Mandela's childhood was unusual because of his early departure from his mother's household and his subsequent upbringing as the ward of a royal regent. Mandela's emotional self-control as a personality, as well as his receptiveness to new ideas, is, I think, attributable to his upbringing in highly institutionalized settings. Both at court and at school, Mandela absorbed principles of etiquette and chivalry that remained important precepts through his public life. They were principles that were reinforced by a sophisticated literary culture that fused heroic African oral traditions with Victorian concepts of honour, propriety, and virtue. From his boyhood, Mandela's life was shaped by ideas or values that were shared by rather than dividing his compatriots, black and white. In this context, the absence in his early life of intimidating or humiliating encounters with white people is significant, and, to an extent, distinguishes his childhood from many other black South African childhoods. (Lodge 2006: vii)

Lodge proceeded to posit that 'I find less of a contrast than other writers between the young Mandela and the older veteran of imprisonment. Generally, in Mandela's career there are no sudden turning points; rather key decisions develop out of lengthy incremental processes of thought, and are often influenced by Mandela's recollections of precedent' (ibid.: viii). This childhood experience emerges in Lodge's understanding of Mandela as a form of apprenticeship. Such an approach that takes into account Mandela's childhood and upbringing is important because it assists in avoiding the crisis of reading Mandela solely from a retrospective perspective informed by hindsight. But the weakness of Lodge's emphasis on absence of turning points in Mandela's life made him fail to appreciate various antinomies that haunted his life.

At the time of the death of Mandela, a journalist, Patrick Bulger, warned all those who were reflecting on the legacy of Mandela to be extremely cautious of a number of pitfalls. In the first place, they had to avoid the temptation to mythologize and reproduce Mandela as a flawless hero or even a political saint. In the second place, they had to be careful to avoid creating a 'seamless and perfect life whose unfolding, and whose highs and lows, belong in the realm of what became for South Africa and the world a fairy tale, complete with its own happy ending' (Bulger 2013). Lodge nearly fell into this trap.

Bulger was basically concerned about the pitfalls of analytical wisdom informed by hindsight which often miss the empathetic understanding of the realities faced and confronted by the subject understudy. The second warning came from Slavoj Zizek:

> If we want to remain faithful to Mandela's legacy, we should thus forget about celebratory crocodile tears and focus on the unfulfilled promises his leadership gave rise to. We can safely surmise that, on account of his doubtless moral and political greatness, he was at the end of his life also a bitter, old man, well aware how his very political triumph and his elevation into universal hero was the mask of a bitter defeat. His universal glory is also a sign that he really didn't disturb the global order of power. (Zizek 2013)

But Mandela never claimed easy victories at any time in his political career.

## Antinomies in Mandela's Life

The best way to do justice to the analysis of Mandela's complex life struggle is to see it as constituted by a plurality of antinomies, ambiguities and contradictions, just like that of other freedom fighters. For active political humanists like Mandela, the personal became political too. The celebrated South African historian Philip Bonner (2014: 29–30) identified five antinomies of Mandela. The first was between his early socialization informed by his rural upbringing and the urban and modern life he lived in Johannesburg. How did Mandela reconcile these two influences? It seems he used both influences selectively and strategically as per the situation in the course of his life of struggle. This point is well captured by Zolani Ngwane when he argued: '[t]he winning secret in this masculinist discourse is that the subject is able to negotiate himself out of tradition without making the politically and culturally unpopular choice of 'modernity', but by embedding tradition (or rather, certain modalities of tradition) in the very expression of African nationalism itself' (Ngwane 2014: 116). Mandela like other African nationalists engaged in the creative activity of translating traditional influences and local symbols into usable tools of the nationalist struggle through the deployment of nationalist metaphors pregnant with liberatory messages. Tradition and culture became weapons of the nationalist, decolonial and liberatory struggle. For example, his appearance at the Rivonia Trials donning the traditional Xhosa kaross had a meaning in the context of a people resisting colonial apartheid that pretended to be founded on European modernity. As he put it: 'I had chosen traditional dress to emphasize the symbolism that I was a black African walking into a white man's court' (Mandela 1994: 168).

But Ngwane (2014: 115) highlighted a serious tension if not contradiction in Mandela's relation to tradition and modernity. In the first place, in the early pages of his autobiography Mandela emphasized how he was a child of tradition and custom where '[t]his was the alpha and omega of our existence and went unquestioned' (Mandela 1994: 11). But in 1996 when Winnie Mandela tried to use Xhosa tradition to oppose divorce, arguing that Mandela should have used traditional elders to mediate their disputes, Mandela declared in court that 'I respect custom but I am not a tribalist. I fought as an African nationalist and I have no commitment to the custom of any particular tribe' (quoted in Meredith 1997: 541).

The second antinomy was between family life and political life. Colonialism, particularly its initiation of migrant labour, directly threatened African family life. In South Africa the urban areas were for whites. Male labourers were allowed as per the needs of colonial capitalism. A combination of modern colonial patriarchal ideas and precolonial traditional patriarchy produced and consolidated female domesticity. Africans like Mandela who became active in African nationalist politics became even more prone to sacrifice family for the wider nationalist liberation struggle. Harassment, imprisonment and detention became their political identity. This is why Brenna Munro wrote: 'The unfolding public saga of Nelson Mandela's "private" life, with its marriages, divorces, separations, reunions and bereavements, has been emblematic of the South African experience during apartheid and its aftermath. The personal is political for an icon, and gender performance is an integral part of the theatre of politics' (Munro 2014: 92).

When his wife, Winnie Mandela, also became active in the anti-colonial struggle, family life for the Mandelas collapsed completely. Winnie became the 'mother of the nation' and Mandela the 'father of the nation' (du Preez Bezdrop 2003). These sacrifices also contributed to their eventual divorce in 1996. This is how Anne Marie du Preez Bezdrop captured the political tensions between Nelson and Winnie Mandela: 'Winnie was increasingly critical of Mandela's political outlook, and had been shocked when he described de Klerk as a man of integrity. She argued with Mandela over his view, denouncing de Klerk as no less a murderer than PW Botha. And Mandela's call on ANC supporters in Natal to disarm enraged her' (ibid.: 238).

Different conceptions of the struggle and its possible resolution after Mandela's release from prison caused tensions between the 'mother of the nation' and the 'father of the nation'. The family suffered consequently. The third antinomy was political in nature. Bonner (2014: 29) captured it as 'tension between Mandela's submission to party discipline and his individualistic tendencies'. From the 1950s, the ANC emphasized what became known as the collective. But there were instances where Mandela moved ahead of others for the sake of progress in the liberation struggle: the first was his singular motivation for the shift from the strategy of nonviolence to that of armed struggle, and the second was his individual initiation of negotiations with the apartheid government in the 1980s.

But this can be appraised positively as a product of a leader with a vision, capable of leading from the front when circumstances dictated. This might be linked also to the fourth antinomy of 'tension between Mandela's consistency and his impetuosity' (Bonner 2014: 30) as well as the last antinomy of 'flexibility and intransigency'. These I would argue were informed more by responding to exigencies of the nationalist decolonial struggle and the intransigence of the apartheid regime than by character qualities. How could one expect Mandela to be consistent and inflexible while actively involved as a leader in a struggle that had reached a stalemate that needed various tactics and strategies to break? Mandela had to work actively almost every day of his life to circumvent antinomies, tensions, ambiguities and contradictions, all of which cascaded from various exigencies of the struggle.

## Is Mandela also an Ordinary African Nationalist?

But these tensions, ambiguities, contradictions, vicissitudes and exigencies did not dent or tarnish Mandela's stature as a leading advocate of critical decolonial ethics of liberation. Various lives of Mandela are discernible within which his political formation and making emerged and crystallized. Danny Schechter's *Madiba A to Z: The Many Faces of Nelson Mandela* (2013) dramatizes the various lives of Mandela. The leading African historian Paul Tiyambe Zeleza (2013: 10) posited that the political formation of Mandela and the meaning of his politics as well as legacy 'cannot be fully understood through the psychologizing and symbolic discourses preferred in the popular media and hagiographies'. Zeleza emphasized that Mandela was a political actor within the broader drama of African nationalism and decolonial struggles, concluding that:

Mandela embodied all the key phases, dynamics and ideologies of African nationalism from the period of elite nationalism before the Second World War when the nationalists made reformist demands on the colonial regimes, to the era of militant mass nationalism after the war when they demanded independence, to the phase of armed liberation. (ibid.)

Zeleza (2003) distilled five important humanistic objectives of African nationalism that are discernible in Mandela's life of struggle. The first was the anti-colonial decolonization, the second was nation-building, the third was development, the fourth was democracy, and the final one was pan-African integration and unity. Zeleza added that:

> Reconciliation was such a powerful motif in the political discourses of transition to independence among some African leaders of the imperatives of nation building, the second goal of African nationalism. It was also a rhetorical response to the irrational and self-serving fears of imperial racism that since Africans were supposedly eternal wards of whites and incapable of ruling themselves, independence would unleash the atavistic violence of 'inter-tribal warfare' from which colonialism had saved the benighted continent, and in the post-settler colonies, the retributive cataclysm of white massacres. (Zeleza 2013: 12)

Mandela was, however, not the only African humanist who railed against both racism and reverse racism. The leading African scholar Mahmood Mamdani documents in his *Define and Rule* (2013c: 112) how Julius Nyerere of Tanzania introduced an alternative model of statecraft that sought to dismantle both tribalism and racism in the same manner that Mandela sought to dismantle apartheid colonialism. Like Mandela, Nyerere in 1962 sought to create an inclusive citizenship. Nyerere even stated publicly that:

> If we are going to base citizenship on colour we will commit a crime. Discrimination against human beings because of their colour is exactly what we have been fighting against ... They are preaching discrimination as a religion to us. And they stand like Hitlers and begin to glorify the race. We glorify human beings, not colour. (Quoted in Mamdani 2013: 112–13)

It merits attention though, that the variations in forms of colonialism had a bearing on the forms of nationalism, nature of struggles for decolonization and ideologies. Mandela emerges as 'largely a home-grown pragmatic revolutionary' whose politics was shaped by his location within a country that was organized on a racial basis (Zeleza 2013: 10). The long incarceration further enabled him to reflect carefully on the nature of the racial problem facing his country and the possible solutions. But like all other African political actors, Mandela also fought to transcend some parochialisms imposed on his life by history, tradition and culture.

## Highlights of Mandela's Life History

Below is a condensed summary of the highlights of Mandela's various lives presented in chronological order.

**Figure 2.1** Timeline of Mandela's Life

| 1918 | Mandela was born on 18 July in Mvezo in the Eastern Cape. His father Gadla Henry Mphakanyiswa, chief of the Mvezo, named him Rolihlahla, which means 'agitator'. |
|------|--------|
| 1919 | Mandela family moved to Qunu, north of Mvezo, where Mandela became a herd boy. This experience helped Mandela later in his leadership of the ANC and the people, leading them from behind and exercising 'obedential power' (commanding, while obeying). |
| 1925 | Mandela was now aged 7 and he became the first person in his family to go to a modern school. It was at school that his teacher gave him an English name: Nelson. |
| 1927 | Mandela lost his father, and his mother took him to Mqhekezweni to live at the court of the Tembu paramount chief Jongitaba Dalindyebo. This chief became Mandela's guardian. Mandela took advantage of his new home to observe at close range the exercise of traditional power and the style of traditional Xhosa governance. |
| 1935 | Like all other Xhosa boys of his age, Mandela underwent the traditional custom of circumcision. Soon after this his guardian bought him his first pair of shoes as part of his preparation to go to Clarkebury Boarding School located at Engcobo. It was here that Mandela began to be aware of the world beyond his Xhosa worldview. |

| 1937 | Mandela continued his education, this time at Healdtown, a Wesleyan Methodist Mission School in Fort Beautfort in the Eastern Cape. |
|------|--------------------------------------------------------------------------------------------------------------------------------------|
| 1939 | Mandela began his tertiary education when he registered for a BA degree at the University of Fort Hare, which is the Alma Mater of many leading black politicians. |
| 1941 | Mandela was suspended from the University of Fort Hare for his involvement in a student strike. During this same time he faced the challenge of an arranged marriage. This led Mandela to flee to Johannesburg where he worked as a security guard at a gold mine. It was during this period that he met Walter Sisulu who helped Mandela to get a job as a clerk at a white law firm. Mandela continued with his studies with the University of South Africa (UNISA). |
| 1942 | Mandela graduated with a BA degree. During this time, Mandela began attending meetings of the African National Congress (ANC) together with his Africanist-decolonial mentor, competent mass mobilizer, and friend, Gaur Radebe. |
| 1943 | Mandela started active participation in politics of resistance to colonial rule. He marched alongside Gaur Radebe who had organized ten thousand others in support of the Alexandra bus boycott, a protest against the raising of fares from four to five pence. He also registered for a Law degree at the University of the Witwatersrand while becoming active in ANC politics to the extent of proposing the idea of an ANC Youth League. Mandela was part of a delegation that included Anton Lembede, Peter Mda, Walter Sisulu, Oliver Tambo and William Nkomo that went to see Dr Xuma (ANC President) to introduce the idea of organizing a Youth League. |
| 1944 | Mandela married Walter Sisulu's cousin, Evelyn Mase. During this year the ANC Youth League was formed on Easter Sunday at the Bantu Men's Social Centre in Eloff Street. |
| 1952 | Mandela and his friend Oliver Tambo established the first black-owned law firm in Johannesburg. |

| 1955 | Mandela's marriage to Evelyn Mase deteriorated to the extent that Mase gave him an ultimatum to choose between marriage and the ANC. During this year the ANC adopted the Freedom Charter. |
|---|---|
| 1956 | Mandela was arrested on a charge of high treason, and when he returned home he found that Evelyn Mase had left the house. They officially divorced in 1958. |
| 1958 | Mandela married Nomzamo Winfred Madikizela. |
| 1962 | Mandela was arrested after more than fifteen months on the run. He was sentenced to five years in jail for leaving the country illegally and organizing an illegal strike. |
| 1962–63 | In 1962 Mandela left South Africa illegally to attend the Pan-African Freedom Movement for East, Central and Southern Africa (PAFMECSA) in Addis Ababa, Ethiopia. He underwent military training in Ethiopia. In 1963 Mandela and others' trial at Rivonia began. Mandela's mother Nosekeni and Winnie Mandela came to court to support him. |
| 1964 | Mandela and seven comrades were convicted of high treason in the Rivonia Trial. The state requested the death penalty but they instead were sentenced to life imprisonment. Seven were sent to Robben Island while Dennis Goldberg was sent to Pretoria Central simply because prisons were segregated according to race. Whites were not candidates for Robben Island. |
| 1976 | Mac Maharaj was released from Robben Island and he smuggled out of prison Mandela's autobiography, and that copy became the basis of *Long Walk to Freedom*. |
| 1977 | Winnie Mandela was banished to Brandfort in the Free State. At Brandfort, Winnie continued the fight for the rights of black people and even set up a soup kitchen and started a clinic. |
| 1982 | Some of the Rivonia Trialists were moved to Pollsmoor Prison in Tokai, Cape Town. The conditions here were better than on Robben Island. |

| 1984 | For the first time in twenty-one years, Mandela met his wife and was able to hold her hand and kiss her during a contact visit in Pollsmoor Prison. |
|---|---|
| 1985 | Mandela had his first meeting with the PW Botha government. He met the minister of justice, Kobie Coetsee, while recovering from prostate surgery. He was now at Pollsmoor Prison. |
| 1988 | Mandela was moved from Pollsmoor Prison to Victor Verster Prison in Paarl. Here he stayed in a house with a garden, a swimming pool and a chef. |
| 1989 | Mandela had more regular meetings and contacts with the apartheid government. During this same year, PW Botha had a stroke and was succeeded by FW de Klerk. Mandela's colleagues Walter Sisulu, Raymond Mhlaba, Ahmed Kathrada and Andrew Mlangeni were released from prison.<br><br>The exiled wing of the ANC issued the Harare Declaration that expressed the ANC's willingness to negotiate on condition that the apartheid government release all prisoners, lift the ban on all political formations opposed to apartheid, end the State of Emergency, and remove all the troops from the townships. |
| 1990–91 | On 2 February 1990, at the opening of parliament, President FW de Klerk announced the unbanning of the ANC, Pan-Africanist Congress (PAC) and South African Communist Party (SACP).<br><br>On 11 February 1990, at the age of 71, Mandela was released after spending twenty-seven years in jail.<br><br>In July 1991, at the first Annual Conference of the ANC inside South Africa, Mandela was elected president of the ANC without opposition.<br><br>On 20 December 1991, after more than a year and a half of talks about talks, the Convention for Democratic South Africa (CODESA) began. The talks were boycotted by the PAC and Inkatha Freedom Party (IFP). |

| 1992 | The cracks in Mandela and Winnie's marriage became more obvious. Chris Hani, the former chief of staff of MK and one of the most popular figures in the ANC was assassinated. Two weeks after the assassination of Hani, Oliver Tambo passed on too.<br><br>South Africa's last whites-only referendum was held. White people were asked whether negotiations for a new constitution should go ahead, and 68.7% voted in favour of it.<br><br>CODESA2 kicked off in May 1992 without much progress being made. |
|---|---|
| 1993 | On 3 June 1993, after months of negotiations at the World Trade Centre, the multi-party forum voted to set a date for the country's first national, non-racial, 'one-person-one-vote' election: 27 April 1994.<br><br>On 10 December 1993 Mandela and de Klerk were awarded the Nobel Peace Prize, the most distinguished award made to global peacemakers. |
| 1994 | On 27 April 1994 Mandela voted for the first time at Ohlange High School in Inanda in Durban.<br><br>The ANC polled 62.6% of the national vote and won 252 of the 400 seats in the national assembly.<br><br>On 10 May 1994 Mandela was inaugurated as the first black state president of South Africa. |
| 1996–97 | After thirty-seven years of marriage, Mandela and Winnie divorced in March 1996. Winnie changed her name to Winnie Madikizela-Mandela.<br><br>The Constituent Assembly enacted a permanent constitution.<br><br>In 1997 Mandela announced his plans to step down as the South African president at the ANC's 50th conference at Mafikeng, North West Province. |

| 1998 | The Truth and Reconciliation Commission Report was published.

On 18 July 1998 Mandela married Graca Machel. |
| 1999 | Mandela retired from politics after serving only one presidential term. |
| 2013 | On 5 December 2013 Mandela passed on. |

*Sources*: Mandela, *Long Walk to Freedom* and *You Magazine: Special Issue – Mandela: Man of History. Tribute to SA's Greatest Son, 1918–2013.*

Figure 2.1 highlights some of the major aspects on Mandela's life from childhood to the time of his death. But it is still important to comment and elaborate on some of them, particularly the emergence and growth of his political consciousness. Mandela was born into a Xhosa family. Xhosa custom, ritual and taboo shaped his early life in a profound way. Inevitably, his early mind-map was fixated at Mvezo, Qunu and Mqhekezweni where he was born and grew up. Mandela's formative political consciousness was influenced by what was happening at the 'Great Place' (royal place) of Chief Jongintaba Dalindyebo, the acting regent of the Thembu people. This is clearly articulated by him in his autobiography: 'My later notions of leadership were profoundly influenced by observing the regent and his court. I watched and learned from the tribal meetings that were regularly held at the Great Place' (Mandela 1994: 19).

Chief Jongintaba Dalindyebo had become Mandela's guardian after he lost his father. Mandela therefore grew up a part of a royal family, knowing that he was a Thembu first, and second, a Xhosa. He did not know that he was a South African at that stage of life, it was only when he went to school: 'I began to sense my identity as an African, not just a Thembu, or even Xhosa. But this was still a nascent feeling' (Mandela 1994: 36). Mandela came from a society where even marriages outside his own 'Xhosa ethnic' identity were considered a taboo. Marriages were still being arranged. This might explain why his two former

**83**

wives, namely Evelyn Mase and Winnie Madikizela, were of Xhosa stock. Thus Mandela admits: 'But as I left Healdtown at the end of the year, I saw myself as a Xhosa first and an African second' (ibid.: 40).

It was only after studying at the University of Fort Hare that Mandela claimed to have advanced socially beyond Xhosa parochialism to the extent of rebelling 'against the social system of my people' (ibid.: 52). Mandela admits that he had to learn through travel and exposure that he was a South African who was experiencing racial discrimination and domination, like all others who grew up in rural areas during Mandela's time. Mandela mentions in his autobiography that some prisoners criticized him for always keeping the company of Xhosa-speaking prisoners. He had to grow from this ethnic parochialism into one of the most revered African leaders in South Africa and beyond.

## Development of Mandela's Political Consciousness

The development of Mandela's political consciousness is interesting. Mandela posits that it came naturally because of the circumstances of oppression facing black people. Mahmood Mamdani (1991: 236) once argued that 'without the experience of sickness, there can be no idea of health. And without the fact of oppression, there can be no practice of resistance and no notion of rights'. Mandela's explanation of his political formation and consciousness seem to confirm Mamdani's argument. Mandela stated:

> I cannot pinpoint a moment when I became politicized, when I knew that I would spend my life in the liberation struggle. To be African in South Africa means that one is politicized from the moment of one's birth, whether one acknowledges it or not. An African child is born in an Africans Only hospital, taken home in an Africans Only bus, lives in an African Only area and attends Africans Only schools, if he attends school at all. (Mandela 1994: 89)

Mandela admits that when he left the University of Fort Hare he was advanced socially but not politically. He only developed politically when he reached Johannesburg, 'a city of dreams, a place where one could transform oneself from a poor peasant into a wealthy sophisticate, a city of danger and opportunity' (ibid.: 56). The city life tended to erode strong ethnic distinctions and foster new broader identities and solidarities.

In Johannesburg black people experienced the common problem of racial profiling and racial domination. This condition had the effect of politicizing Africans. This is why Mandela wrote: 'There was no particular day on which I said, henceforth I will devote myself to the liberation of my people; instead, I simply found myself doing so, and could not do otherwise' (Mandela 1994: 89). Being an African in a racist society made African people to be political. Mandela was further influenced by a number of people whom he met in Johannesburg, such as Walter Sisulu, Anton Lembede, and many others.

What is worth noting is that Mandela's early political consciousness was deeply nationalistic. He rejected communism. He also rejected the involvement of Indians and whites in African politics. As he puts it: 'At the time, I was firmly opposed to allowing communists or whites to join the league' (Mandela 1994: 94). He elaborated that during the heyday of the ANC Youth League: 'I was sympathetic to the ultra-revolutionary stream of African nationalism. I was angry at the white man, not at racism. While I was not prepared to hurl the white man into the sea, I would have been perfectly happy if he climbed aboard his steamship and left the continent on his own volition' (Mandela 1994: 106).

Besides his activism and leadership within the ANC Youth League, by 1952 Mandela had entered the centre of top ANC leadership when he was appointed first deputy president to Chief Albert Luthuli. But his first position in the ANC came in 1947 when he was elected to the executive committee of the Transvaal ANC. This meant that Mandela became exposed to banning, endless appearances in court, and imprisonment. By then Mandela had noted that he was 'more certain in those days of what I was against than what I was for' (Mandela 1994: 112). It was also a time for Mandela to reflect and revise some of his political convictions. He began to study works of Marxism and Leninism which resulted in him changing his opposition to communism without changing his nationalist bona fides.

His frontline leadership included the drawing of the M-Plan that would ensure the continued existence and operation of the ANC in the event it was banned. Part of the M-Plan included political lectures on 'The World We Live In', 'How We are Governed', and 'The Need for Change' (Mandela 1994: 135). Mandela also took the initiative to critique the strategy of non-violence, and became an advocate for counter-violence as a future strategy of the ANC. His idea was that 'non-violence was not a moral principle but a strategy; there was no moral goodness in using an ineffective weapon' (ibid.: 147). Mandela strongly believed that '[t]o overthrow oppression has been sanctioned by humanity and is the highest aspiration of every free man' (ibid.: 151). It was the experience of how the apartheid government responded to the Defiance Campaign that provoked Mandela to see no alternative to armed and violent resistance. His conclusion was this: 'A freedom fighter learns the hard way that it is the oppressor who defines the nature of the struggle, and the oppressed is often left no recourse but to use methods that mirror those of the oppressor. At a certain point, one can only fight fire with fire' (ibid.: 155).

Mandela was therefore not a typical Gandhi character, though his life of struggle and legacy had deep elements of Gandhism. The intransigence and violence of apartheid could not be dealt with by using Gandhian tools only. They were not adequate to the task at hand. Mandela took singular leadership in motivating for the establishment of uMkonto we Sizwe ('The Spear of the Nation') as a military wing of the ANC in the post-Sharpeville period. His determination was demonstrated by his underground work and the risks he took, which earned him the name 'Black Pimpernel'.[1] Mandela's approach to armed struggle and use of violence still distinguished him as a humanist because there was emphasis on not endangering human life. The ANC never sanctioned military attacks on whites as legitimate targets of the nationalist struggle. The struggle had to target symbols of white privilege, supremacy and domination. Sabotage was a preferred tactic of the anti-apartheid struggle. Future reconciliation of races was envisioned from the beginning; hence the liberation struggle was not reduced to a 'blood-feud between whites and blacks' (Mandela 1994: 170).

Mandela also distinguished his leadership and commitment to the liberation of South Africa when he left the country illegally in 1962 to mobilize support for the armed struggle. To that extent, he even underwent military training in Ethiopia. The experience he gained through his travel on the continent was that African leaders were suspicious of ANC's cooperation with liberal whites, Indians and communists. Mandela's solution was that the ANC must feature prominently within the Congress Alliance as the effective leader of Africans (Mandela 1994: 294). Even though Mandela was soon arrested when he arrived back in South Africa, he continued to demonstrate courage and leadership. He clearly understood what his life symbolized: 'I was the symbol of justice in the court of the oppressor, the representative of the great ideals of freedom, fairness and democracy in a society that dishonoured those virtues. I realized then and there that I could carry on the fight even inside the fortress of the enemy' (ibid.: 299). By the time of the Rivonia Trials Mandela had become a public symbol of justice, resistance and struggle. The imprisonment of Mandela and others on Robben Island did not fully succeed in robbing the fighting people of South Africa of leadership. The long imprisonment of Mandela contributed in a big way to the making of a global icon. Mandela became a macrocosm of the anti-colonial and anti-racist struggle as a whole. But as stated by Mandela, the intention of the apartheid regime was to use imprisonment to undermine the anti-colonial and anti-racist forces' struggle and resolve. This is how he put it: 'Prison is designed to break one's spirit and one's resolve' (ibid.: 373–74).

Within prison Mandela continued to play a leading role as the spokesperson for all prisoners. Oliver Tambo took over the presidency of the ANC after the death of Chief Albert Luthuli. It is not given though that if Mandela was not incarcerated he was going to automatically become the president of the ANC. What is clear is that the long imprisonment boosted his image as the face of anti-apartheid resistance in South Africa. Mandela spent eighteen years on Robben Island and he used that time to develop an even deeper understanding of the problems facing South Africa and their possible resolutions. He entered prison as a radical and emerged from it as a voice of reason and moderation. He entered prison at the age of 44 and was released at the age of 71. Mandela had now assumed a mythical stature within anti-colonial and anti-racist political formations. He became a 'living' martyr of the liberation struggle. On the impact of imprisonment on one's character, Mandela wrote that '[p]erhaps it requires such depths of oppression to create such heights of character' (Mandela 1994: 609). Mandela's friend Archbishop Desmond Tutu's reflections on the impact of imprisonment on Mandela are that

> Prison mellowed him wonderfully. As you know, he went to prison a very angry, youngish man. I mean, the commander-in-chief of the military wing of the ANC, so he was pretty aggressive ... But had he come out earlier, we would have had the angry, aggressive Madiba. Suffering either embitters you or, mercifully, ennobles you. And with Madiba, thankfully for us, the latter happened. He grew in his magnanimity. He became able to put himself in the shoes of the other ... When he came out, only someone like him could have said to – especially these young angry types – that no, we've to go for negotiations. (Quoted in Schechter 2013: 13–14)

Imprisonment features prominently in the pedigree of African nationalist struggles. Part of the narrative of African nationalist struggles is that nationalist leaders emerge from prison straight to state house. It happened with Kwame Nkrumah and Jomo Kenyatta. Leaders like Joshua Nkomo and Robert Mugabe of Zimbabwe languished in detention for a decade. Mandela's political story is therefore indeed part of these African nationalist struggles and histories. This is why Anthony Sampson (2000: 495) wrote that '[t]here was nothing new in Africa about prisoners suddenly coming to power: from Nkrumah in Ghana and Kenyatta in Kenya to Mugabe in Zimbabwe – all had faced unfamiliar problems'.

But one can also argue that, at another level, Mandela's long imprisonment made him part of a project of those in control of the apartheid state. This was clear when they could suddenly remove him from Robben Island to Pollsmoor Prison in 1982 and then to Victor Verster Prison in 1988. Mandela could not be ignored in any of the political schemes of the beleaguered apartheid regime. The scheme involved isolating him from his fellow political prisoners. The second part was to offer him preconditions for release. But this scheming opened the possibilities for a negotiated settlement. Even more importantly, Mandela effectively took advantage of the overtures from the beleaguered apartheid regime to push for political change at every stage of the encounters.

While in his autobiography Mandela creates the impression that he initiated the negotiations with the apartheid government, the reality on the ground indicates that the exiled ANC under OR Tambo had been seized with the complex issue of negotiations since the 1980s. The leading black South African historian Sifiso Mxolisi Ndlovu (2010: 63), in his detailed backgrounding of the ANC and negotiations, defined the 1980s as 'the age of reason, where the trajectory of South African society was characterized by absorbing intellectual battles and ideas on majority rule, constitutional guidelines and the meaning of a non-racial, democratic South Africa'. Ndlovu provides details of the genesis of 'talks about talks' dating back to 1984 when journalists and highest opinion makers in South Africa and the world began approaching the ANC through OR Tambo. By 1985, Tambo had already instructed Thabo Mbeki to prepare and submit to the ANC National Executive Committee (NEC) a report on the question of negotiations. Mbeki indeed submitted a document entitled 'A Submission on the Question of Negotiations' in 1985 (Ndlovu 2010: 66). Ndlovu credits the ANC's multi-pronged revolutionary strategy for forcing the apartheid government to the negotiating table. The revolutionary strategy was predicated on four pillars: all-round vanguard activity of the underground structures of the ANC; the united mass action of the peoples; the armed offensive spearheaded by Umkonto we Sizwe; and finally, the international drive to isolate the apartheid regime (ibid.: 64).

But this background must not be read as an attempt to counter Mandela's claims to have initiated another front of negotiations from the perspective of a prisoner who was not in exile. Thus in justifying his individual initiative to initiate negotiations with the apartheid regime, Mandela stated that '[t]here are times when a leader must move out ahead of the flock, go off in a new direction, confident that he is leading his people the right way' (Mandela 1994: 510–11). Opening up individual negotiations with the apartheid regime was very risky. Mandela risked being misunderstood by the ANC both inside and outside South Africa. The second bigger risk was well captured by Danny Schechter (2013: 28): 'He was one man up against an adversary with a whole bureaucracy behind it'. As stated by Ndlovu (2010: 75), the 'apartheid regime adopted a divide-and-rule strategy on the question of negotiations by offering to release Mandela' in the first instance. But thanks to Mandela's strong political consciousness and deep commitment to the ANC, he stood on a high moral and humanistic pedestal and managed to gradually gain the confidence of his adversaries and the support of the progressive world, without compromising the liberation struggle.

In initiating the negotiations, Mandela was in the process transforming his political identity from what the apartheid regime regarded as a terrorist and prisoner to that of a negotiator and facilitator of 'talks' between the ANC and the apartheid regime, complementing the initiatives that were already underway in exile. Through his initiative, Mandela contributed to pulling off one of the most challenging, significant and unexpected transitions from apartheid colonialism and authoritarianism to democracy.

But there were a number of other factors besides Mandela's leadership that enabled negotiations. The celebrated historian Leonard Thompson (2001: 241–43) noted that while the apartheid regime was trying to use the state of emergency to contain opposition to apartheid, other factors undermined the regime's long-term prospects. The first factor was demographic. The white population had dropped from the peak of 21 per cent of the total population in 1936 to 15 per cent in 1985. According to Thompson, the 1998 official estimates were that by the year 2005 whites would form only 10 per cent of the population. The second factor was economic. The South African economy was experiencing a deep recession. This was caused by a combination of the impact of sanctions and the militancy of workers. The third factor was that the apartheid regime's dogma of segregation of races was proving to be a myth and a fantasy in the context of the realities of interdependence of blacks and whites. The end of the Cold War also contributed to the demise of apartheid. These factors however do not minimize the role played by Mandela and, to some considerable extent FW de Klerk, in bringing about transition in South Africa.

But what emerges poignantly from this chapter is firstly that Mandela's biography and even hagiography is that of the shifting idea of South Africa and changing redefinition of the contours of the liberation struggle. The second issue is that of a Mandela who used his long-term incarceration at Robben Island to think deeply about the planetary idea of the human. Once confined to an island and to a very small cell, Mandela meditated deeply about why some human beings purposefully dehumanized others. The outcome of this meditation, it would seem, was a Mandela who was dedicated to save humanity from dehumanization. To him, it would seem, the architects of apartheid were fallen human beings who needed to be rescued and liberated from the politics of racism and hate. This is why we find Mandela working actively as the first black president of South Africa to invite erstwhile racists back into humanity through symbolic acts including polishing PW Botha's shoes. All these were symbolic acts of demonstrating love rather than hate in the true spirit of decolonial humanism.

The next chapter analyses and evaluates how the negotiations that produced the transition to democracy in South Africa were informed by a new logic of justice that was superior to the Nuremberg template. It details the factors that enabled the transition, in the process highlighting the complex historiographical debates that emerged on the question of negotiations in general, and CODESA in particular.

## Notes

1. This name was taken from the Baroness Orczy's fictional character the Scarlet Pimpernel, who daringly evaded capture during the French Revolution.

# Three

# Mandela at CODESA, and New Conceptions of Justice

## Introduction

> Courageous people do not fear forgiving, for the sake of peace.
> – Nelson Mandela quoted in Sampson, *Mandela:*
> *The Authorised Biography*

> A nation struggling to be born faced the dilemma of laying the
> ghosts of a dark past to rest with neither retributive justice nor
> promotion of a culture of impunity. How much success could be
> expected? How would we manage the inevitable fall-out from those
> demanding more justice before reconciliation?
> – Mamphela Ramphele, *Laying Ghosts to Rest*

> History is in most cases a reflection of the views of victors and
> of those with the power to impose their version on those who
> have been conquered or are in less powerful positions. In the
> case of South Africa there are neither victors nor vanquished.
> We have a contested history.
> – Mamphela Ramphele, *Laying Ghosts to Rest*

The time of the negotiations was the most complicated for the
liberation forces and the most difficult for Mandela as the catalyst
of transition from apartheid to democracy. It has produced its own
historiography that is enlightening pitting those who privileged
the importance of global geopolitical power terrain and those who
privileged internal factors and the contribution of the liberation

forces towards forcing the apartheid regime to the negotiating table. The global terrain had shifted from Cold War to neo-liberalism. The Soviet Union that had sponsored the ANC had collapsed. Communism as an ideology has been discredited. The long liberation struggle had raised high expectations. The apartheid regime had been delegitimized but was still militarily stronger than the liberation forces. Among the liberation forces there was no clear consensus on the merits of negotiations. The diehard and unrepentant racists were eager to derail the transition. Representatives of local and global capital had their own agenda which saw them engaging in parallel secret negotiations. The setting was indeed complex. During this same period the ANC had to reorganize itself into a modern political party embracing ex-exiles, ex-prisoners and those who were spearheading the struggle from inside South Africa. Black-on-black violence was sponsored and escalated as part of a broader agenda to derail the negotiations and forestall the transition. Mandela had to demonstrate leadership within this complex context.

## The Complex Setting for Negotiations

Sifiso Mxolisi Ndlovu, a leading black South African historian who played an active part in the writing of the South African Democracy and Education Trust (SADET) multi-volume book series on the South African road to democracy in his analysis of the countdown to the Convention for a Democratic South Africa (CODESA) of 1991, views negotiations as a culmination of 'the traditional intellectual battle of minds that commenced in the early twentieth century between the South African National Native Congress (SANNC, later renamed the ANC) and the whites-only Union of South Africa government' (Ndlovu 2013: 723). To Ndlovu, the genealogy of the struggles for an inclusive and sovereign convention to deal with the South African national question must be traced back to the two conventions of 1908 and 1909: the first being 'the racist, whites-only 1908 convention that presaged the 1902 Treaty of Vereeniging. The second took place in 1909 and was organized by the founders of the ANC who opposed the establishment of the racially governed Union of South Africa' (Ndlovu 2013: 724).

Ndlovu's central argument is that '[t]he question of substantive negotiations in South Africa, defined by diplomacy and peaceful talks in the late twentieth century, flows organically from earlier history'. He documents in detail the initiatives take by Africans since 1909 to find peaceful solutions to the South African national question. These involved sending deputations to Britain as the colonial power, and a ceaseless call for a national convention, including the writing of letters to apartheid regime leaders explaining the need for one. For example, on 20 April 1961, Mandela wrote a formal letter addressed to Prime Minister HF Verwoerd, proposing a national convention for the peaceful resolution of the South African national question whose subset the colonial and apartheid regime rendered as the 'native question' (Ndlovu 2013: 727). When South Africa was descending towards a republic, again Mandela actively engaged the white colonial regime over the necessity of a national convention. For example, on 23 May 1961 Mandela wrote another letter, this time to De Villiers Graaff (the leader of the white opposition party) calling for a national convention:

> In one week's time the Verwoerd government intends to inaugurate its republic ... the decision has been taken by little over half of the White community: it is opposed by every articulate group amongst African, Coloured and Indian communities, who constitute the majority of this country ... we have called on the government to convene an elected national convention with the task of drawing up a new constitution for this country which should be acceptable to all racial groups ... But where, Sir, does the United Party stand? We have yet to hear ... from you, its leader ... It is time for you, Sir, and your party, to speak out ... Are you for a democratic and peaceable solution of our problems? Are you, therefore, for a national convention? We in South Africa and the world outside expect an answer. Silence at this time enables Dr Verwoerd to lead us onwards towards the brink of disaster. (Nelson Mandela's letter quoted in Ndlovu 2013: 728)

Ndlovu noted that '[t]he dispute about convening a national convention in a racially divided South Africa continued throughout the twentieth century' (ibid.: 729), with the white-dominated regime ignoring the calls. Consequently, Ndlovu is of the view that CODESA is the culmination of long-standing demands led by the ANC for a peaceful resolution to the South African national question through an inclusive and sovereign national convention. He therefore identified four major factors that set the stage for CODESA:

(1) The liberation movement gaining ascendancy over the apartheid regime, both internally and internationally. All the pillars of the ANC's struggle for national liberation were going from strength to strength. A very high level of mass mobilization and mass defiance had rendered apartheid unworkable. The apartheid regime could neither resist fundamental change nor guarantee the long-term security of the white population. The building of the underground struggle had laid a basis for political leadership, and there was international solidarity of action against apartheid.

(2) At the same time the liberation movement faced certain major weaknesses because changes in the southern African political architecture were making it difficult for the ANC to intensify the armed struggle. The international community, particularly the Western superpowers, were renewing their attempts to interfere with internal issues affecting South Africa.

(3) The crisis in Eastern Europe and the resultant changes in the relations between world powers brought the issue of a negotiated settlement in South Africa to the fore. Importantly, these changes also exerted new pressure on the apartheid regime to fall in line with emerging international 'culture' of multi-party democracy and majority rule.

(4) The apartheid power bloc was no longer able to rule in the old ways. Its politics of repression and reform had failed dismally; and it faced an ever-deepening socio-economic crisis. Economically, apartheid became unaffordable as the economy contracted and this reduced the resources available for the apartheid regime to fight against the liberation movements and simultaneously pursue the imperial war against Angola. It is also true that the liberation movement did not have the immediate capacity to overthrow the apartheid regime. (Ndlovu 2013: 743)

Ndlovu's analysis is important as it provides a counterbalance to those scholars who emphasize the contribution of external factors. Ndlovu's other important point is that he disputes the popular view of the ANC being 'a lackey of the Soviet Union and the Communist Party of South Africa (later renamed the SACP)'. To him,

[t]he argument ... is not convincing and has to be jettisoned. This is because the ANC founders such as Seme, Mapikela, Dube, Rubusana and Plaatjie began their quest to address the national question in South Africa during the convention of 1909 and 1912, and CODESA was convened 82 years later. This was also several years before the Soviet Union became a reality and an entity. The ANC leadership and supporters also fought for freedom, human rights and democracy before the CPSA was established in South Africa. Furthermore, the efforts by white liberals to claim easy victories regarding the 1996 Constitution should be dismissed as opportunistic because the ANC insisted that a Bill of Rights should be enacted in 1923. The national movement did not need permission from both the communists and white liberals when they took this groundbreaking decision. A Bill of Rights was finally enacted in the 1996 Constitution for a democratic South Africa. (Ndlovu 2013: 794)

However, the leading South African economist Sampie Terreblanche, who played a role in the secret negotiations that eventually delivered a democratic transition in South Africa in 1994, emphasized the role of external factors and identified '[t]he year 1986 as the real turning point in South Africa's democratic transformation'. To him, the democratic transition that took place in South Africa 'was not an isolated event but part of a major reconfiguration of the world's power constellation that was institutionalized after the Second World War'. He elaborated that '[t]he South African transformation was not the result of the Cold War. Rather, the fall of apartheid and the Soviet Union were separate but interrelated consequences of this major global reconfiguration of power in the decades after 1980 and in which the United States played a leading role' (Terreblanche 2012: 7).

Terreblanche identified four important geopolitical conjunctures that enabled the South African transition. The first was the explosion at the Chernobyl nuclear power plant in the Soviet Union on 26 April 1986, which revealed Soviet incompetence and consequently hastened the end of the Cold War as Michael Gorbachev 'realized how badly the Soviet Union had regressed and how much it needed to cooperate with the Western world'. The second event was President PW Botha's declaration of a comprehensive state of emergency on 12 June 1986 that revealed not only that 'South Africa was governed by military and police generals known as the securocrats' but also his 'desperate attempt to prolong the lifespan of the apartheid regime' (Terreblanche 2012: 10).

The third event was the acceptance by the United States Congress of the Comprehensive Anti-Apartheid Act in October 1986 that authorized the institution of sanctions, boycotts and disinvestments policies against South Africa. The last one was the Reykjavik Summit between Ronald Reagan and Michael Gorbachev of 11–12 October 1986 in Iceland during which Reagan revealed the ability of the United States of America to launch a supercomputer microchip military revolution; this compelled Gorbachev to abandon his country's superpower aspirations as well as military and financial support to various military groups including the ANC (Terreblanche 2012: 12–13). The leaders of the two superpowers agreed to work together towards 'finding negotiated and diplomatic solutions for all the important flashpoints in the world', and these included the South African apartheid problem, the Namibia–Angola–Cuba problem, the Israel–Palestine conflict; the India–Pakistan conflict, the problems in Northern Ireland, and the North Korean problem (ibid.: 15).

Britain under Margaret Thatcher also got actively involved in finding a solution to the South African apartheid problem, beginning with sending the Eminent Persons Group (EPG) to South Africa in 1986 and inviting President FW de Klerk to London on 23 June 1989 where she delivered to him the message from the 'Great Powers' to the effect that Britain would no longer continue with its non-sanctions policy and advised him to release Nelson Mandela from prison before the end of 1989 so as to begin negotiations between the apartheid government and the ANC (Terreblanche 2012: 15–16).

All this indicates that global forces played a catalytic role in pushing the South African disputants to the negotiating table. But this argument does not by any means seek to down play the role of internal forces or of Mandela himself in bringing about the South African disputants to the negotiating table. Terreblanche's analysis of the forces that were active in pushing for the transition is illuminating in a number of ways. It highlights those forces that are often ignored in the analysis of the complexities of the transitional politics. As an economist he highlights the important role played by the Mineral Energy Complex (MEC). This is how he put it:

> When the NP government declared the general state of emergency in June 1986, and when the American Congress enacted the Comprehensive Anti-Apartheid Act in October 1986, the South African business sector realized that their crisis of accumulation was very serious and became convinced that a transition to a political dispensation that would include the ANC had become inevitable. (Terreblanche 2012: 59)

The business sector began to toy with difficult questions of how to persuade the ANC and other anti-apartheid forces to abandon their socialist orientations; how to influence the ANC away from adopting a nationalist populist posture as a post-apartheid government that would entail agendas of nationalization of commanding heights of the economy as well as massive redistribution of land and social spending; how, importantly, to ensure that the ANC would not deviate from the economic status quo in which capitalist corporations, monopolies and oligopolies were dominant; how to persuade the National Party (NP) government, particularly its radical conservative racist fringe of the Afrikaners, of the necessity and inevitability of negotiations and a negotiated settlement involving the African liberation forces as being the only solution to the crisis of South African apartheid; and finally, how to reign on the militant trade union movement, particularly the Congress of South African Trade Unions (COSATU), to tone down its ideology for a proletarian revolution (Terreblanche 2012: 59; Habib 2013).

Terreblanche's analysis of the forces involved behind the scenes included the influence of United States' neo-liberal advocates and architects of the Washington Consensus. This is why in the latter part of the 1980s the MEC succeeded in persuading the NP government to accept neo-liberalism, including adoption of policies of privatization. This was followed in 1990 by the South Africa Chamber of Business publishing Economic Options for South Africa, which was a positive response to the dogma of neo-liberal globalism (Terreblanche 2012: 60). To prove that the NP government had converted to neo-liberal dogma, it published its Normative Economic Model (NEM) as its economic blueprint for a democratic South Africa.

The important point is that those who were operating within the MEC played a significant role in issuing a warning to both the ANC and NP government while influencing them to negotiate and reform apartheid in a way that did not threaten the economic dominance of the MEC. Important business personalities such as Harry Oppenheimer worked on Mandela throughout the early 1990s. What is also important to emphasize is that while CODESA meetings were taking place in public in Kempton Park, corporate leaders had parallel and secretive negotiations that took place at the Development Bank of South Africa (DBSA) aimed at influencing the economic policy of South Africa. Terreblanche (2012: 63) writes that '[d]uring these meetings an elite compromise gradually emerged between the WTA (under the leadership of the MEC), a leadership core of the ANC, and American and British pressure groups'. He adds: 'In fact, we ought to feel rather sorry for the ANC because all other participants in the secret negotiations – the local and foreign corporate sectors, the National Party, the American and British pressure groups – were ideologically committed to neoliberal globalism and market fundamentalism. The strongest foreign pressure on the ANC, in all probability, came from American pressure groups' (Terreblanche 2012: 64).

According to Terreblanche (ibid.: 73), the secret negotiations involving the leaders of the corporate sector working in cohort with American pressure groups was to produce a post-apartheid South Africa that was 'a satellite of the American-led neo-liberal empire'. This arrangement had no space for possibilities of a radical and comprehensive redistribution policy which was expected from the ANC by its majority black constituencies. It had an impact on negotiations, as Terreblanche (ibid.: 69) posited: 'One possible scenario is that the NP deliberately slowed down the CODESA negotiations to give the MEC enough time to box in the ANC with an elite compromise on economic issues'. The ANC indeed became 'lost in transformation', and the efforts of Mandela to create a racially inclusive and people-centred society and a 'rainbow nation' were frustrated by secret negotiations that maintained the economic status quo. Indeed the DBSA secret negotiations focusing on economic policy resulted in a suspension of the revolution, which affected the quality of the Kempton Park political negotiations.

## The Politics of CODESA Negotiations

The negotiations that culminated in the historic 27 April 1994 elections were marked by pitfalls and setbacks. At the same time the options for South Africa were either to negotiate or risk a racial bloodbath. This difficult choice was eloquently captured by Robert Schrire's *Adapt or Die: The End of White Politics in South Africa* (1991). But the apartheid regime and the so-called 'third force' were still embedded in the paradigm of war, and there were also hardliners in the African National Congress who were still confident of a military victory. A number of incidents took place that sought to derail the negotiations.

The first was the Sebokeng massacre in which the apartheid police opened fire on protesters and killed eleven of them (Thompson 2001: 248). This behaviour of the apartheid police did not indicate any paradigm shift conducive to the continuation of negotiations. Inevitably, the ANC immediately suspended the talks with the apartheid government. It was Mandela who broke the ice by requesting a private meeting with President FW de Klerk. The meeting resulted in the signing of the Groote Schuur Minute of May 1990 that was informed by a recommitment to negotiations, a lifting of the state of emergency, and a joint task force to remove further stumbling blocks to negotiations.

During this time, the ANC was reluctant to accept the idea of ending the armed struggle, which was a condition put by the apartheid government for negotiations to continue. The ANC demanded the release of all political prisoners, the return of exiles, and the removal of the state of emergency in line with the Harare Declaration of 1989. The intervention of Joe Slovo of the SACP convinced the ANC National Executive Committee (NEC) to end the armed struggle (Ottawa 1993; Waldmeir 1997). These concessions produced the Pretoria Minute of August 1990. But violence continued to haunt the preparations for negotiations. The ANC and Inkatha Freedom Party (IFP) supporters continued to kill each other in what became known as 'black-on-black' violence, which was most pronounced in KwaZulu-Natal province. The ANC suspected that the apartheid government had a hand in these violent incidents. Again Mandela negotiated an agreement with the IFP leader Gatsha Mangosuthu Buthelezi on January 1991. But violence continued, prompting Mandela to state that '[b]efore the ink was even dry, the blood was flowing again. I began to believe, more and more, that the government was behind the violence' (Mandela quoted in *You Magazine: Special Issue on Mandela*, April 2014). The unrepentant fringe of the Afrikaner community was another problem as they even went to the length of trying to physically disrupt the negotiation proceedings by driving cars into the venue.

But Mandela continued to play a leadership role in making sure those forces bent on destroying the negotiations – that is, those who were struck in the paradigm of war – were dealt with and invited to the negotiation table. His initiatives resulted in the signing of a national peace treaty with de Klerk and Buthelezi. In a typical humanist spirit Mandela had made an impassioned speech aimed at persuading Buthelezi and his IFP to embrace the paradigm of peace: 'I will go down on my knees to beg those who want to drag our country into bloodshed and to persuade them not to do so' (Mandela 1994: 536). This humility produced a peace treaty. This peace treaty opened the way for the First Convention for a Democratic South Africa (CODESA) that took place on 20 December 1991.

Mandela had this to say about this breakthrough: 'After more than a year and a half of talks about talks, the real talks began. We had taken our future into our own hands and, as fellow South Africans, we were settling our differences among ourselves' (Mandela quoted in *You Magazine*, April 2014). The historian Leonard Thompson also highlighted the importance of CODESA when he wrote:

> CODESA opened on December 20, 1991, in the World Trade Centre outside Johannesburg. It was strikingly different from the National Convention of 1908/09, when thirty white men created the Union of South Africa out of four British colonies, with a flexible constitution that enabled the white minority to establish a system of racial domination. CODESA comprised nearly three hundred delegates, most of them Africans, many of them women. (Thompson 2001: 252)

Still there were problems. Nineteen political parties sent 228 delegates, but the Conservative Party (CP), the PAC, the Azania People's Organization (AZAPO), and the leader of the IFP boycotted the event but sent a delegation. Despite these problems, CODESA II kicked off on 15 May 1992, though marred by differences. The apartheid regime was demanding the dismantling of uMkonto we Sizwe, the military wing of the ANC. Violence was still a major problem, and the lives of many people, mainly black, were being lost on a daily basis in the townships. The clear example was the Boipatong Massacre of 17 June 1992. The range of other problems included the role of the public broadcaster SABC, the carrying of traditional weapons, the prosecution of political criminals, and the nature of interim government. At the time of the convening of the Multiparty Negotiating Forum (MPNF) on 1 April 1993, new challenges had arisen. The first was the assassination on 10 April of Chris Hani, the popular leader of the SACP and a former chief of staff of uMkonto we Sizwe, and the second was the storming of the World Trade Centre by the extreme right-wing Afrikaner Weerstandsbeweging that was opposed to the negotiations (Thompson 2001: 256).

These were provocations that were meant to defeat the spirit and substance of negotiations. But the signing of the Record of Understanding restored hope. Fear and despondency were replaced by optimism once more. Credit goes to Mandela, and de Klerk to some extent, for making sure the negotiations continued. The interventions of Joe Slovo also assisted the process, particularly his wisdom on sunset clauses. In the end, all the major political formations participated in the historic elections of 27 April 1994 that produced a democratic dispensation. This background is important to take into account before one can venture into a critical analysis of the essence of the CODESA negotiations.

## The Essence of CODESA and a New Paradigm of Justice

Chandra Lekha Sriram and Suren Pillay, in *Peace versus Justice? The Dilemma of Transitional Justice in Africa* (2009), articulate two dilemmas facing transitional justice and peace-building in general. The argument is well captured by Chandra Lekha Sriram in particular who writes:

> The so-called peace versus justice dilemma arises following violent conflict, in which victims and their families, local and international non-governmental organizations (NGOs), and other actors in the international community often demand that some form of accountability be imposed on the perpetrators of gross human rights violations and war crimes. Those calling for accountability frequently insist that it must be pursued for the sake of victims, their survivors, society at large, deterrence and the (re)building of democracy and the rule of law. Those seeking to promote peace-building (a broad range of activities to ensure that conflict does not re-emerge) may concur that there is value in seeking accountability, but raise concerns that it may destabilize fragile post-conflict societies. These two positions often form the poles of the so-called peace versus justice debate. (Sriram 2009: 1)

Sriram, however, posits that '[t]his dichotomous dilemma is often overstated'. This is so because '[i]n reality the choice is seldom simply "justice" or "peace" but rather a complex mixture of both' (ibid.). At CODESA, the ANC and Mandela faced this dilemma practically. They had to be creative in trying to address the needs and demands of victims, perpetrators, winners and losers. This is why CODESA was rearticulated as aiming at transcending the

**103**

paradigm of war and opening the way for the creation of a post-apartheid society. The paradigm of war has in human history given birth to Nuremberg trials as a template of justice. But at CODESA what was being negotiated was a new paradigm of peace with a potential to produce a kind of political justice amenable to the political reform of society.

As argued by Mamdani (2013a, 2013b), the Nuremberg paradigm of justice is predicated on the logic that violence should be 'criminalized without exception, its perpetrators identified and tried in a court of law'. On the other hand, the CODESA paradigm of justice became predicated on a different and particular thinking on mass violence as political rather than criminal, which suggested the re-making of political society through political reform as a lasting solution (ibid.). At the centre was a drive to transcend a paradigm of war and conceptions of justice as predicated on criminal justice involving the punishment of certain individuals. A paradigm of war is sustained by an unending circle of production and reproduction of perpetrators and victims in which today's perpetrator becomes tomorrow's victim, and vice versa. But Suren Pillay provides a more complex normative expectation that complicates the push for a paradigm of peace without justice. He argues that

> the need for 'justice' as a normative expectation frames much of our contemporary legal, political and ethical vocabulary. We inhabit a world in which justice itself has become normalized as a right enshrined in a cache of legal instruments. We also think of wrongs committed against us, as individuals and collectivities, through the prism of justice, framing these forms of 'injustice'. Inherent to this sentiment is the almost naturalized view that, when a wrong is committed, justice *has to be done or at least must be seen to be done*. The kind of justice to which we refer here concerns what might constitute the proper response to a wrong. The prevailing ethos that has shaped the 'proper' response to a wrong in the Western world has been influenced by the notion of *lex talionis*: 'an eye for an eye'. (Pillay 2009: 347)

Pillay goes on to argue that that indeed 'many states around the world do still take life for life in the form of the death penalty'. At the same time, 'in conflicts within and between states there has been a shift away from "victor's justice" and the encouragement of reconciliation between hostile parties' (ibid.). There are concerted efforts to rearticulate transitional justice in a new way in which it remains 'a form of justice that seeks to be a response to a wrong at the same time seeking to be a form of justice [that] avoids the legal absolutism of retributive justice' (ibid.: 349).

It was in this spirit that South African liberation stalwart and legal scholar Kader Asmal explained the logic behind the South Africa compromises reached at CODESA:

> We must deliberately sacrifice the formal trappings of justice, the courts and the trials for an even higher good: Truth. We sacrifice justice because the pains of justice might traumatize our country or affect the transition. We sacrifice justice for truth so as to consolidate democracy, to close the chapter of the past and avoid confrontation. (Asmal quoted in Verwoed 1997: 19)

It would seem that the Mandela who was working together with other stalwarts of the struggle like Joe Slovo was fully committed to trying something new in the domain of transitional justice. In fact, the situation of a political stalemate needed political innovation and creativity to unblock it. The stalemate was crisply captured by Mamdani (2013a: 6) in these words: 'neither revolution (for liberation movements) nor military victory (for the apartheid regime) was on the cards'. Mandela led the ANC into CODESA fully aware that it was another 'theatre of struggle, subject to advances and reverses as any other struggle' (Mandela 1994: 577). History was not on the side of the apartheid regime. Apartheid had far outlived its life as a form of colonialism. It had survived the decolonial winds of change of the 1960s and 1970s, but it could not survive the post-Cold War normative discourses of democracy and human rights. One can even say the post-Cold War dispensation was more favourable to Mandela's initiatives. But the ANC had also lost its major ally in the form of the collapse of the Soviet Union. This is why Mamphela Ramphela in *Laying Ghosts to Rest* explained the transition this way:

> Our transition to democracy is anything but a miracle. The tree of freedom in South Africa was nourished by the blood of many martyrs over the years of struggle. It benefited from the fall of the Berlin

**105**

Wall and the shift in geopolitics. It is a product of careful strategic leadership of Nelson Mandela and others. Its road was paved by the extraordinary sacrifices of all those who fought for freedom at home and abroad. It was made easier by rituals and symbols that helped victims and perpetrators of human rights abuses to face up to the ghosts of the past and make peace with them. (Ramphela 2008: 45)

The points raised above are reinforced by Frank B. Wilderson who argues that it took major tectonic shifts in the global paradigmatic arrangement of white power, such as the fall of the Soviet Union which was the major backer of the ANC, the return of forty thousand black bourgeoisie exiles from Western capitals and a crumbling global economy 'for there to be synergistic meeting of Mandela's moral fibre and the aspirations of white economic power' (Wilderson 2010: 8). Indeed imperatives and interests of white capitalists who were experiencing the biting effects of sanctions and popular unrest at home played an important role in influencing the negotiators.

But it is clear that what Mandela wanted and demanded from the apartheid regime was the dismantlement of apartheid and a commitment to a non-racial, democratic and free society. He sought to achieve this through the following strategy: 'To make peace with an enemy, one must work with that enemy, and that enemy becomes your partner' (Mandela 1994: 598). His overriding intention was to banish once and for all apartheid oppression, hence in his inaugural speech as the first black president of South Africa in 1994 he emphasized: 'Never, never, and never again shall it be that this beautiful land will again experience the oppression of one by another ... The sun shall never set on so glorious a human achievement. Let freedom reign. God Bless Africa!' (Mandela 1994: 607).

Building on the earlier argument by Mamdani (2013a) of how South Africa's transition to democracy was predicated on a paradigmatic shift from the post-Second World War Nuremberg form of justice founded on criminal justice, one ineluctably arrives at a favourable evaluation of CODESA. It was not merely a time of betrayal of decolonial liberation struggle through compromises, but CODESA embodied another form of justice. This reality was well captured by Mamdani who wrote:

Whereas Nuremburg shaped a notion of justice as *criminal* justice, CODESA calls on us to think of justice as primarily *political*. Whereas Nuremberg has become the basis of a notion of *victim's justice* – as a complement to victor's justice [rather] than a contrast to it – CODESA provides the basis for an alternative notion of justice, which I call *survivor's justice*. (Mamdani 2013a: 2)

Mamdani went on to elaborate on the differences between criminal justice and political justice in this way:

> CODESA prioritized political justice over criminal justice. The difference is that criminal justice targets individuals whereas political justice affects entire groups. Whereas the object of criminal justice is punishment, that of political justice is political reform. The difference in consequence is equally dramatic. The pursuit of political justice requires that you decriminalize the other side. This means to treat the opponent as a political adversary rather than as an enemy. This makes sense only because the goal is no longer to punish individual criminals, but to change the rules and thereby reform the political community. Morally, the objective is no longer to avenge the dead but to give the living a second chance. (Mamdani 2013a: 7)

The way the ANC and Mandela dealt with conflict generated by apartheid colonialism had broader implications for how to interpret, comprehend and resolve intractable social conflicts in Africa in particular and in the world at large. This was inevitable because the South African settlement and transition to democracy took place at the end of the Cold War. The end of the Cold War not only witnessed the 'norming' of democracy and human rights as global values but also the outbreak of many identity-based conflicts including the shocking Rwandan Genocide in 1994.

As noted by Adam Habib (2013: 235), the scholarly and policy debates pertained to the trade-offs made between civil and human rights on the one hand, and historical redress and systemic reform on the other. Mamdani above has taken the lead in recommending survivor's justice as opposed to the victor's justice as an alternative way of resolving intractable conflicts in postcolonial Africa. His widely discussed and debated book *Saviours and Survivors* (2009) focused the conflicts that have rocked Sudan for a long time. It is a treatise of how survivor's justice as opposed to victor's justice would be useful in resolving Africa's intractable conflicts.

Mamdani's perspective is justified on the basis of the case studies of South Africa and Mozambique where, according to him, intractable conflicts were resolved through negotiations in which disputants were not further bifurcated into perpetrators and victims. The problem that arises with this innovative intervention is that in the first place, by raising the perpetrators and victims to the same level, there is a danger of being seen as underplaying the abrogation of human rights and the suffering of citizens. It would seem in this scheme of things that the perpetrators benefit at the expense of victims, just for the sake of living together. Adam Habib (2013: 240) posed two fundamental questions in his critique of Mamdani's push for survivor's justice: 'Under what terms and conditions should individual justice be tempered for survivor's justice?' and 'Beyond making a theoretical case, under what conditions does survivor's justice become a real possibility and how can these conditions be created?'

The response is that this happens where the conflict has reached a stalemate and where 'peace is to be the collective dividend' (Habib 2013: 240). Ideally, as noted by Habib (ibid.: 243) a simultaneous pursuit of immediate human rights and historical redress would work better. But the question is, under what terms and conditions can this be possible? The South African situation did not make that possible as part of negotiations. There were complex power questions to be sensitive to. These included the fact that the apartheid regime, despite its illegitimacy, had a military capacity that far exceeded that of the liberation movements combined. The ANC had legitimacy and global support because apartheid had long been identified as an inhuman system. There was also the corporate sector which used its economic leverage to retain enormous influence while conceding very little to the demands of the liberation movements. Then there were labour movements with their capacities to strike and their support for the ANC (Habib 2013: 27–29).

Ahmed Kathrada (2011), a stalwart of the liberation struggle and a close associate of Mandela, argued that '[n]ot a single individual in government ranks, nor even in the liberation movement, had the stature of Madiba, and no one else could have commanded the respect needed to avert disaster' during the course of the negotiations. Kathrada is particularly fascinated by the way Mandela exercised leadership in the wake of the assassination of Chris Hani, which had happened just a year before the 1994 elections, and which threatened to plunge the country into a bloodbath. Mandela rushed from the Transkei to Johannesburg and assumed a leadership role that the then President FW de Klerk's government was failing to do. Mandela used the power of rhetoric to save the nation from disaster:

> Tonight I am reaching out to every single South African, black and white, from the very depth of my being. A white man, full of prejudice and hate, came to our country and committed a deed so foul that our whole nation now teeters [on] the brink of disaster. A white woman, of Afrikaner origin, risked her life so that we may know, and bring to justice, this assassin ... Now is the time for all South Africans to stand together against those who, from any quarter, wish to destroy what Chris Hani gave his life for – the freedom of all of us. (Mandela quoted in Kathrada 2011: 1)

According to Ari Sitas (2010), Mandela engaged in 'indigenerality', which he elaborated as a set of inclusive discourses of the 'rainbow nation' encompassing the liberal, ecclesiastical discourse of forgiveness that made possible the negotiations to end apartheid (see also Hart 2013: 7). These discourses found deeper symbolic and substantive expression in the Truth and Reconciliation Commission's rituals.

## The Truth and Reconciliation Commission (TRC) and the Past

The decolonial humanist anti-apartheid struggle was not meant to punish the ideologues of apartheid but to destroy the edifice of apartheid itself. On the ashes of juridical apartheid, the ANC and Mandela envisaged a new post-racial and pluriversal political community founded on new humanism and inclusive citizenship. If one closely reads Mandela's autobiography and critically assesses his political actions after taking over as the first black president, one finds a leader who was aware that through negotiations and the Truth and Reconciliation Commission (TRC) only one battle was partially won – that of legislating administrative apartheid out of existence. As noted by Ramphela (2008: 46), the TRC did its ritual of 'laying ghosts of the dark past to rest with neither retributive justice nor promotion of a culture of impunity'. But according to Mamdani (2013a: 13), the TRC escaped the Nuremberg trap 'by displacing the logic of crime and punishment with that of crime and confession'.

Having said this, Mamdani went on nonetheless to distil how the TRC was still influenced by the Nuremberg template of justice, particularly in its definition of a victim and a perpetrator. In the first place, victimhood was individualized alongside the individualization of the responsibility of the perpetrator (Mamdani 2013a: 13). This had two immediate implications and one long-term implication. The first was that a human rights violation was consequently narrowly defined 'as an action that violated the bodily integrity of an individual' (ibid.). This was problematic in a situation where structural violence was the most pervasive DNA of the apartheid system.

The second implication was 'obscuring the fact that the violence of apartheid was mainly that of the state, not individual operatives' (Mamdani 2013a: 13). The long-term implication was that the narrow definition of both victim and perpetrator created an ideal environment to avoid dealing with the pertinent question of social justice and structural socio-economic transformation (Mamdani 2002). Most of the energy was spent in finding an immediate way of creating a viable post-apartheid political society in which those who had survived apartheid hailing from across the political divides could have a chance to lead a new life.

One can argue that while CODESA made commendable efforts to transcend the limitations of Nuremberg, the TRC did not extend this paradigmatic shift forward. Although the TRC acknowledged that apartheid was a 'crime against humanity', it did not put it on trial beyond this acknowledgement. The TRC did not go to the roots of the human wrongs that were introduced by colonialism and apartheid that produced conflict, war and violence. The TRC inevitably degenerated to a statistical methodology that highlighted symptoms of the conflict and then apportioned blame to particular organizations that were categorized as 'perpetrator organizations' and 'victim organizations'. This point is well put by Mahmood Mamdani (2010):

> The TRC undertook a statistical analysis of the victims and perpetrators of this crime 'against humanity'. In the process, it reached some strange conclusions. To begin with, it argued that most of the violations under apartheid, roughly over half, had occurred during the period of transition from apartheid, and not during apartheid proper. The TRC then tabulated the affiliations of all victims and perpetrators as two separate lists, one of 'victim organizations' was headed by the ANC; then followed the IFP, with the South African Police (SAP) in the 7th place, and down the list, followed the Azania People's Organization (AZAPO). When it came to 'perpetrators organizations', the IFP was ranked first and the ANC third; and the South African Police (SAP) was placed second, and the South African Defence Force (SADF) fourth. (Mamdani 2010: 6)

The TRC consequently never put apartheid as a colonial system on trial, with a view not to prosecute and punish but to mark a paradigmatic shift from historical wrongs into a new era of social transformation and political reform that was emerging from CODESA. Instead it seemed to decriminalize apartheid as a system, a system that authorized what Mamdani (2010: 9) termed 'extra-economic coercion', including dispossession, forced removals, and displacements. The agenda of economic and social justice was consequently not put on the agenda as a necessary socio-economic project:

> Had the TRC acknowledged pass laws and forced removals as constituting the core social violence of apartheid, as the stuff of extra-economic coercion and primitive accumulation, it would have been in a position to imagine a socio-economic order beyond a liberalized post-apartheid society. It would have been able to highlight the question of justice in its fullness, as not only criminal and political, but also as social. The step the TRC failed to take is the challenge South Africa faces today. (ibid.: 10)

This point is also raised by Ramphela (2008: 50) who argued that the TRC, by '[f]ocusing on gross violations of human rights, meant that violations of socio-economic rights of the disfranchised majority were left unexamined'. Mandela is consequently criticized for failure to deal effectively with the pertinent question of economic and social justice. The TRC was meant to do this but it failed. It ended up as a mere performance if not a theatre that was bereft of social content. This character of the TRC was partly due to its leadership by the cleric Archbishop Desmond Tutu, who was prone to perform the ritualistic elements at the expense of the substance. According to Thompson,

> the TRC did not advance the cause of racial reconciliation. Indeed, in the short run it had the opposite effect, accentuating the racial divisions in South African society. Nor did the TRC bring justice to the victims of political violence. Many killers and torturers walked free for talking about their crimes, and victims received little compensation from the reparation committee. (Thompson 2001: 278)

If this critique is taken seriously, it means that the TRC failed to deliver even if assessed on its own narrow terms and remit that avoided socio-economic justice. In any event the TRC tended to benefit those people who committed gross violations of human rights in the name of the apartheid system, if only because the apartheid regime ended up being treated as though it was a legitimate government operating according to legitimate laws.

Ramphela (2008: 63) noted that what also emerged as a major challenge from the TRC was what she termed 'The dilemma of moral equivalence relating to crimes committed by both sides to the conflict'. It rationally boggled the minds of those who had risked their lives to fight against apartheid to find themselves being put on the same moral standing and test regarding crimes with those who had fought on the side of an apartheid regime that was now being condemned by the whole world for committing crimes against humanity. Ramphela posed penetrating questions:

> Is it fair that the liberation movements were asked to come clean about the atrocities they committed in the name of the struggle against apartheid? Does the right to defend oneself against an unjust order not make for a just war? Do the combatants in a just war

face the same moral test for their actions in engaging the enemy?
(Ramphela 2008: 63)

But Joel Netshitenzhe (2012) explained the logic of the negotiations and the settlement from the perspective of the ANC: 'At the
risk of oversimplification, it can be argued that a critical element
of that settlement, from the point of view of the ANC, was the
logic of capturing a bridgehead: to codify basic rights and use
these as the basis for more thoroughgoing transformation of South
African society' (ibid.: 16).

Building from this logic, it would seem, it was clear to Mandela
and the ANC that the transformation of society was never going
to be an event but a process. Perhaps a strong confidence in the
morality of decolonial humanism made the ANC and Mandela
naive, even to the extent of expecting those who had benefited
from apartheid economically to be immediately reborn into new
compassionate human beings capable of acknowledging the historical grievances of those who had been abused and dispossessed
by apartheid to the level of voluntarily committing themselves to
play an active and voluntary part in the equal sharing of resources
with those who had been dispossessed and exploited by apartheid
colonialism.

Netshitenzhe reinforces the argument that decolonial humanism
drove the way Mandela and the ANC imagined a post-apartheid
South Africa. He argued:

> The articulation of the ANC mission by some of its more vision-
> ary leaders suggests an approach that, in time, should transcend the
> detail of statistical bean counting and emphasis on race and explic-
> itly incorporate *the desire to contribute to the evolution of human
> civilization. At the foundation of this should be democracy with a
> social content*, excellence in the acquisition of knowledge and the
> utilization of science and *a profound humanism*. (Netshitenzhe
> 2012: 27; my emphasis)

But concretely speaking, the year 1994 marked not only the end
of administrative apartheid but more importantly the beginning of
a difficult process of nation building which was always tempered
with a delicate balancing between allaying white fears and attending to black expectations and demands. This reality became a

major test of the plausibility and praxis of decolonial humanism. CODESA and the TRC, despite their limitations, were creative and innovative initiatives meant to enable a new post-apartheid pluriversal society to emerge in which all humanity would regain their ontological density. However Mamdani has highlighted the difficulties involved in what Mandela was trying to create. This is how he put the challenge:

> In the context of a former settler colony, a single citizenship for settlers and natives can only be the result of an overall metamorphosis whereby erstwhile colonizers and colonized are politically reborn as equal members of a single political community. The word reconciliation cannot capture this metamorphosis ... This is about establishing, for the first time, a political order based on consent and not conquest. It is about establishing a political community of equal and consenting citizens. (Mamdani 1998: 5)

If, as put by Thompson (2001: 278), despite CODESA and TRC, 'race continued to be the basic line of division in South African society, with class becoming increasingly significant among blacks', how did Mandela try to build an inclusive South Africa in concrete terms?

## The Mandela Presidency and His Efforts at Nation Building

Any assessment of the Mandela presidency (1994–99) risks the temptation of privileging a remarkable biography, an exceptional personality, and the humanism of Mandela, in the processing missing an appreciation of the concrete intractable challenges that faced South Africa at the time Mandela took over the reins of power in May 1994. These challenges included the integration of the defence forces (SADF) into a single South African National Defence Force (SANDF) and harmonizing the education system that had been fragmented into 'nineteen separate education departments' under apartheid (Thompson 2001: 266).

The restructuring of the army involved 65,000 regular soldiers, ANC guerrillas estimated to number 27,000, Azanian People's Liberation Army (APLA) and PAC guerrillas estimated to number

6,000, and defence forces from the four 'independent Homelands' that numbered approximately 10,000 (Thompson 2001: 272). The police force too had to be harmonized into a single national South African Police Service, as it was fragmented into eleven different agencies (ibid.: 273). The challenges extended to bringing closure to an exceptionally violent society – even the TRC did not succeed in bringing social peace – and dealing with the intractable socio-economic problem of inequality. When Mandela took office, the government coffers were in a very bad state and his government had to service a huge apartheid debt. What also needed immediate attention was the issue of deracializing state institutions in line with the ethos of an inclusive society and a spirit of rainbowism.

But the emphasis here is on how Mandela practically moved in the direction of implementing a decolonial humanist vision of a post-racial pluriversal society. At the core of this vision was the need to take concrete steps to mark a departure from racism towards a deeper appreciation of the importance of difference. In this vision, difference was not interpreted in terms of superior and inferior races. It was interpreted in terms of pluriversality and rainbowism.

Maldonado-Torres (2008a: 126) argued that in decolonial humanist revolutions the appreciation of human difference had to be informed by a humanistic 'interest in restoring authentic and critical sociality beyond the colour-line'. This point was also articulated by Lewis R. Gordon (1995: 154), who posited that 'the road out of misanthropy is a road that leads to the appreciation of the importance of difference'. Apartheid was a worse form of misanthropy founded on 'bad faith'. It had to be transcended by all means, including symbolically.

Mandela was therefore correct to predicate his presidency on symbolic moves aimed at practically allaying the fears of the whites, which involved hailing the erstwhile racists into a new South Africa. Nation building through use of symbolic gestures and other means, including sporting events, dominated Mandela's presidency.

Thus as the first president of the new post-apartheid South Africa, Mandela made it 'his highest priority to lay the

**115**

foundations of a united nation while respecting the cultures of its different racial and ethnic elements' (Thompson 2001: 274). The Afrikaners who had over the years developed a strong nationalism to the extent of institutionalizing apartheid had to be placated as they contained some dangerous extremists who were opposed to the transition. Mandela made this group his priority, to allay their fears. Some Afrikaner extremists had even attempted to wreck the negotiations physically, led by their extremist leader Eugene TerreBlanche.

To win this minority back to the new South Africa, Mandela invested a series of highly publicized symbolic acts. These involved him visiting the 94-year-old widow of Hendrik Verwoerd, who was identified as the ideologue of apartheid and its architect, as well as ex-president PW Botha, despite him having refused to appear before the TRC. Mandela visited them in their homes. He also agreed to the erection of a statue in remembrance of Verwoerd. He had dinner with General Johan Willemse, the former Robben Island commander, and took lunch with Percy Yutar who was the prosecutor during the Rivonia Trial in which Mandela was sentenced to life imprisonment (Thompson 2001: 274). Still continuing with his symbolic offensive, Mandela wore the Springbok jersey and walked onto the field after South Africa won the World Cup against New Zealand. The Springbok rugby team has long been a source of pride for the Afrikaners (ibid.). Kermit E. Campbell argued that

because Mandela chooses not only to exact no retribution against perpetrators of apartheid but also to embrace a key symbol of their dominance, that is, the national rugby team the Springboks, he appears in many ways to embody the Ciceronian ideal orator/ statesman: one who possesses the requisite good character for artful speaking. (Campbell 2012: 48)

As a result of Mandela's effective use of the symbolic in his nation-building initiative, John Carlin wrote a book entitled *Playing the Enemy: Nelson Mandela and the Game that Made a Nation* (2006). During his presidency, Mandela demonstrated a rare ability and awareness of the motivations of his audiences and tried frantically to appeal to their interests as well as the interests of the new nation that he was creating. He proved to be a very shrewd political calculator and a competent manipulator if not persuader of his enemies into his side. The challenge he faced was that he had to be careful to balance appealing both to the fears of whites and the frustrations of blacks.

His critics thought he was bending backwards too much to appease the white minority constituencies at the expense of attending to the interests of his majority black people who voted him into power. While these criticisms had a basis, it would seem Mandela's idea was to ensure that indeed the erstwhile 'settlers'/'citizens' and the erstwhile 'natives'/'subjects' were afforded enough room to be reborn politically into consenting citizens living in a new political society where racism was not tolerated (Mamdani 2001: 63–70). Mandela went further to appeal to the white staffers of the previous apartheid regime at the presidency to stay on and work for his new administration. It would seem Mandela was indeed using every single brick available to build the rainbow nation.

It was also Mandela who argued for the integration of the apartheid national anthem (*Die Stem*) into the new national anthem of the new post-apartheid South Africa. This is how he justified his action: 'The song that you treat so easily holds the emotions of many people who you don't represent yet. With the stroke of a pen, you would take a decision to destroy the very – the only – basis that we are building upon: reconciliation' (Mandela quoted in Carlin 2006: 147). It is clear that Mandela was, according to Campbell (2012: 60), 'a keen discerner of the human soul. He especially came to understand the Afrikaner soul because during the many years that he was imprisoned he studied the Afrikaner prison guards, their language, Afrikaans, and Afrikaner history'. He advised the National Executive Committee of his ANC that to win people to the party 'you don't address their brains, you address their hearts' (Mandela quoted in Carlin 2006: 60). All these efforts were meant to build an inclusive, non-racist, non-discriminatory South Africa, where people from different races and ethnicities would live together harmoniously. The ideology of rainbowism was expected to bind the post-apartheid country together. The concept of the rainbow nation was first coined by

Archbishop Desmond Tutu. It was later developed by Mandela into a South African national ideology.

At the core of the rainbow nation ideology is the characterization of diverse South African people united in diversity by common struggles for life and against apartheid. It is meant to celebrate the country's racially and culturally diverse population as a gift from God and as an inherent social strength. The achievement of the Mandela presidency was to enshrine this ethos of rainbowism into the South African constitution. But a nation cannot just be brought into existence as a product of legislation. The idea of a rainbow nation had to be given life and lived by people for it to be assessed as a success story. The South African national flag symbolized the spirit of rainbowism. Practically, South Africa remained haunted by the ghost of racism. Economic inequalities did not assist in the realization of a rainbow nation.

## Mandela and the Economy

Policy-wise, Mandela's regime became synonymous with the socialist-oriented Reconstruction and Development Programme (RDP). The policy document was crafted by the Economic Trends Group (ETG) that was founded in 1986 at the suggestion of the Congress of South African Trade Unions (COSATU) and comprised leftist and union-oriented academics. It worked with the Macro-Economic Research Group (MERG) that was founded in 1991 on the recommendation of Canada's International Development Research Centre (IDRC) (Peet 2002: 69–70). The RDP was composed of six principles: an integrated and sustainable programme; a people-driven process; peace and security for all; nation building; the linking of reconstruction with development; and the democratization of South Africa (ibid.: 70). The RDP became a very popular policy document which spoke to the expectations of the previously disenfranchised black majority. It promised a 5 per cent economic growth rate for South Africa and the annual creation of 300,000 to 500,000 non-agricultural jobs (Government of the Republic of South Africa 1994: 21). It would seem that where the RDP was effectively applied it worked very well for the poor; for example, in the five years following its adoption, three million people received safe and clean drinking water from the taps within 200 metres of their houses (ibid.: 71). The RDP was promising to be the nerve centre of building a democratic, redistributive, and even socialist-oriented post-apartheid South African society. Also remembered as a legacy of the implementation of RDP were the low-cost houses that are today known as 'RDP houses'.

What has often been missed by those who simplistically blamed the so-called 'class of 1996 neo-liberals' for the abandonment of the RDP and the adoption of the Growth, Employment and Redistribution (GEAR) is the state of the South African economy at the time Mandela took office. The reality that emerges from narratives of those who were in government is that South Africa was simply bankrupt. The closure of the Johannesburg Stock Exchange for two days in 1985 was a symptom of a national economy in deep trouble. Foreign debt was escalating phenomenally. The costs of financing war in Namibia and Angola, the sanctions, and the running costs of funding the ten Bantustans/ Homelands became unsustainable and eroded the treasury.[1] With this background in mind, it becomes clear that the adoption of GEAR had to be done as part of Mandela's personal practical approach to the financial crisis that was bedevilling the national economy.[2]

What is clear though is that GEAR was one form/version of a Structural Adjustment Programme (SAP), as it emphasized economic growth and the attraction of foreign investment rather than redistribution that was emphasized under the RDP. The poor were said to benefit indirectly through the trickle-down effect from successful economic growth. Nothing has so far trickled down to the poor in a substantive way. But Richard Peet (2002) explained the change of policy from RDP to GEAR as having been forced on the ANC by what he termed 'academic-institutional-media (AIM) complexes' working on behalf of a global hegemonic discourse of neo-liberalism – the same forces that made the ANC abandon the policy of nationalization. AIM is composed of business organizations, academics, media, and international financial institutions

– mainly the World Bank and the International Monetary Fund (IMF).

By the time Mandela exited power in 1999, no substantial socio-economic transformation had taken place. The ANC was pursuing a neo-liberal economic path. But Mandela was adamant that his government had laid a solid foundation for the future. He admitted though that '[t]he long walk is not yet over. The prize for a better life has yet to be won' (Mandela quoted in Thompson 2001: 287). But the act of leaving power after serving only one presidential term boosted Mandela's stature as a politician who conceived politics as a vocation rather than as a bureaucratic profession. At the time Mandela left power he was still popular, whereas many of his colleagues across postcolonial Africa were clinging on to power and engaged in unlawful amendments of the constitutions to perpetuate their stay in office. Mandela demonstrated exceptional commitment to the decolonial humanist struggle through enduring twenty-seven years in prison, hailing the erstwhile racists back to the nation, and setting another good example by leaving power voluntarily after serving only one presidential term.

In conclusion, it is clear that the historical, political and diplomatic drama in which Mandela played an important part was very complex, and is subject to various historiographical interpretations without necessarily diminishing his role. This is why it is important to avoid a biographical approach to the understanding of the Mandela phenomenon. Understanding the broader historical, political and diplomatic context as well as geo-political dynamics is very necessary because Mandela was at once a product of this complex context as well as a leading political actor at its centre, shaping it in a particularly pluriversal, decolonial humanist direction.

## Notes

1. Thanks to Professor Sifiso Mxolisi Ndlovu for his written comments giving insights on the interviews he did with those who were closely involved with the economic issues of South Africa.
2. Professor Sifiso Mxolisi Ndlovu argued that 'Mandela had to stand up and be counted, and did not consult' on the question of GEAR.

# Epilogue

# In Search of a Paradigm of Peace

We, the people of South Africa, declare for all our country and the world to know:

That South Africa belongs to all who live in it, black and white, and that no government can justly claim authority unless it is based on the will of the people.
– The Freedom Charter 1955

The decolonial attitude marks a point of departure from the modern natural racial and colonial attitude, as it also involves self-questioning, openness, and a declaration of availability towards those whose humanity has been questioned by modern multiple colonizing and dehumanizing processes.

Throughout all the struggles that have afflicted, and still afflict, the existence of the entire species, one mysterious fact signals itself to our attention. It is the fact that an invisible chain links all the members of humanity in a common circle. It seems that in order to prosper and grow human beings must take an interest in one another's progress and happiness, and cultivate those altruistic sentiments which are the greatest achievement of the human heart and mind.
The doctrine of the equality of the human races, which consecrates these rational ideas, thus becomes a regenerative doctrine, an eminently salutary doctrine for the harmonious development of the species. Ultimately, it evokes for us the most beautiful thought uttered by a great genius, 'Every man is man', and the sweetest divine instruction, 'Love one another'.
– Joseph-Antenor Firmin, *The Equality of the Human Races*

I began this book with a discussion of the need to understand the Mandela phenomenon as a particular form of consciousness cascading from the experience of 'walking through the shadow of death' – an invention of modernity/imperiality/coloniality. I therefore deployed critical decolonial ethics of liberation to understand the Mandela phenomenon as an embodiment of humanism and a search for a paradigm of peace. I then proceeded to point out that Mandela must be approached as an encapsulation of a decolonial civilizational project that was ranged against the Euro-North America-centric modernity, particularly its racist discourses that enabled hierarchization of human population according to race while at the same time authorizing such inimical processes as the slave trade, imperialism, colonialism, apartheid, neo-colonialism and underdevelopment. Mandela's iconic status crystallized and consolidated within a modern world that was bereft of humanness, goodness, love, peace, humility, forgiveness, trust and optimism. It was a world dominated by the paradigm of war, racism and use of the Nuremberg template of justice as a form of conflict resolution cascading from mass violence. Apartheid was a centrepiece of the paradigm of war. Mandela provided an antidote to the paradigm of war. He introduced the paradigm of peace, reconciliation, and racial harmony.

This is why after his death on 5 December 2013 the media became awash with tributes, reflections and reminiscences on what the Mandela phenomenon meant; what he symbolized; and what he stood for. This book has proven that, at one level, Mandela symbolized a deep and unwavering commitment to the liberation of black people from the scourge of racism to the extent of being prepared to die for the cause of decolonial humanism and its values of democracy, human rights, social peace and equality. At another level, Mandela signified what Thandika Mkandawire (2013: 3) termed a 'sane relationship to power'. At yet another level, Mandela embodied a rare commitment to democracy and rule of law to the extent that Mkandawire was compelled to write: 'In a sense Mandela normalized the idea of democracy in Africa'. All these were but part of the agenda of critical decolonial ethics liberation.

But the idea of Mandela and his symbolism also resonated across the globe. The historian Paul Tiyambe Zeleza posited that Mandela at the global level epitomized 'global moral authority, of humanity at its best, the last in the hallowed canon of twentieth century saintly liberators from Mahatma Gandhi to Martin Luther King' (Zeleza 2013: 10). Indeed Mandela's iconic status emerged within the complex, heroic and epic decolonization struggles of the twentieth century; and, living to the age of 95, he came to symbolize post-Cold War struggles for democracy too.

However, Mandela has also been heavily criticized for putting forward his own personal diplomacy that backed up his formation as a global icon while neglecting concrete transformation of South Africa. Radical scholars like Frank B. Wilderson (2010: 11–13) even accused Mandela of being a sell-out who squandered the revolutionary potential of the ANC and ignored the Freedom Charter as he compromised in favour of local white and global capital. The rebuttal is that the balance of forces did not allow Mandela enough room to manoeuvre because he was dealing with an undefeated enemy. Mandela had inevitably to pursue a middle road through and through in the hope that in future white hegemony would be dismantled. He eventually fell into the Nkrumahist idea of seeking the political kingdom first in the hope that the economic kingdom would be added later.

At the time of Mandela's death, the economic kingdom was still an undelivered chimera. This raises the fundamental and perennial question of whether Mandela's iconic status is based on the reality that he never destabilized the modern Euro-North American-centric order of power. The African historical record indicates that those who dared to seek to change the Euro-North American global power architecture like Kwame Nkrumah, Patrice Lumumba and Thomas Sankara, to mention a few, became victims of either military coups d'état or assassinations. Mandela lived into old age, perhaps because he exited power after only serving one presidential term. But by consistently railing against the ideology of race, Mandela was indeed destabilizing the Euro-North American-centric global power structure in which race has remained as an organizing principle since 1492.

But beyond the disavowal of race, this book has demonstrated that the best way to understand Mandela is as an advocate of decolonial ethics of liberation and a symbol of the paradigm of peace and unity informed by profound humanism. His persona must not be understood in *sui generis* but as a roving and changing one in tandem with the shifting schemes of the apartheid proponents, the changing demands and experiences of leading the liberation struggle and shifting global politics. The struggle he was engaged in had a civilizational remit involving the restoration of humanity to those who had been written out of the human ocumene by global imperial designs and colonial matrices of power, as well as inviting those who had embraced the paradigm of war to the extent of falling from humanity back into pluriversal humanism. This concluding chapter therefore provides an understanding of the broader challenges that Mandela faced as one of the freedom fighters from the Global South who were engaged in what I termed the third humanist revolution informed by decoloniality.

## The Logic of Alterity and Egocentrism

The first challenge was that of alterity and its fault-lines. The logic of alterity is founded on egocentricism, which is both mother and father to ethnocentrism(s). Eurocentrism is one of the numerous forms of ethnocentrism. The result has been the poisoned chalice of race and its long-term consequences that Mandela and other anti-colonial freedom fighters engaged as part of their search for a paradigm of peace. These long-term consequences could be summarized as 'paradigm of difference'. Racism is a central organizing principle of alterity and paradigm of difference. Therefore at the core of the constitution of the modern world is racism as an organizing principle. Since the dawn of modernity, racism has been mutating and assuming different markers that seek to conceal it. Today, racism exists and operates like 'witchcraft', which is denied even by 'witches' themselves while it remains hanging in people's minds like a nightmare. We can, therefore, speak of 'racecraft' as we seek to dramatize how racism is even denied by racists who practise it on a daily basis.

Myths of racism nourished the dream of a world without others. Chinweizu (1975) articulated the idea of a world without others in terms of the binary he used as the title of his book, *The West and the Rest of Us*. The 'rest of us' refers to those people who were said to have been 'discovered' by the West and whose humanity was subjected to a series of questions that constituted the grand 'imperial Manichean misanthropic skepticism' (Maldonado-Torres 2007: 245). Race played a central role in the construction of the post-1492 Euro-North American-centric modernity. As pointed out by Nelson Maldonado-Torres, modern racism is constituted by 'a certain skepticism regarding the humanity of the enslaved and colonized sub-others' and 'stands at the background of the Cartesian certainties and his methodic doubt'. The decolonial humanist revolution that is detailed in the chapters of this book is concerned with reversing and eradicating once and for all the imperial/colonial logic of alterity, and banishing the politics of apartheid that institutionalized and naturalized it.

## The Myth of a World without Others

The imperial/colonial logic of the politics of alterity has produced the myth of 'a world without others' in the minds of colonial ideologues. Decolonial humanists have consistently been opposed to this imperial myth, which is a product of post-1492 modern racism. It became a driving force for the colonizer's model of the world and the Eurocentric myth of the existence of empty lands outside of Europe and North America (Blaut 1993). But the idea of a world without others is a misnomer because the very essence of human history is predicated on diversity and the plurality of identities. Inevitably the notions of a world without others became a fertile discursive terrain for racism, nativism, xenophobia, Islamophobia, anti-semitism, tribalism, sexism, patriarchy and ethnicity.

What needs to be understood are the various logics and numerous consequences of the myth of a world without others. In this logic, a racist believes in a world where people of his or her own race live, without others. A xenophobe believes in living in a space without others. A tribalist wishes to live in a world dominated by his or her own tribesmen and women. A nativist believes in a world of natives only. A sexist privileges his or her own sexual orientation as the norm. An ethno-centricist believes in a world without other ethnic groups. A religious fundamentalist believes that his or her chosen religion is the only true religion and justifies the eradication of other religious beliefs. A patriarch believes in the rule of men over women and the exclusion of women from power.

All these markers of alterity magnify the dangers of believing in a world without others and a world that is governed according to asymmetrical power structures and relations. The long-term consequences of the ideas of a world without others include epistemicides and genocides. These actions have accompanied imperialism, colonialism, and present global coloniality. Reflecting on this idea of a world without others, the Nigerian novelist and Nobel Laureate Wole Soyinka concluded that:

> [t]he rise of extreme nationalism, often developing into outright xenophobia, barely disguised under legislative formalisms that never name their real goal – exclusion – is a symptom of the increase, not decrease, of the we-or-they mentality that appears to be sweeping across the globe. It has resulted in wars of varying degrees of bloodiness and low-intensity ... These are wars whose roots, however traceable to histories of repression and competition for various resources, are nonetheless products of the exclusivist narrowness of vision among peoples, and Africa cannot be held to be exceptional. (Soyinka 2012: 9)

Broadly speaking, a world without others is dominated by what Frantz Fanon (1968) termed 'perverse logic'. It is logic not only of oppression and repression, but one of distortion, disfigurement and destruction of histories of those people found outside the Euro-North American world. The Kenyan novelist Ngugi wa Thiong'o (2012: 38) correctly captured the spirit behind the idea of a world without others in these revealing terms: 'Your past must give way to my past, your literature must give way to my literature, my way is the high way, in fact the only way'. What is at play in a world without others is the narrow ego-politics of being alone in the world.

Thus the Mandela phenomenon spoke and speaks to the broader existential paradox that has faced black people since the dawn of Euro-North American-centric modernity in 1492 and the subsequent colonial encounters of the sixteenth century. It is a paradox facing those human beings who were/are part of the modern world but were/are structurally outside of it, engaged in a lifetime struggle to reverse those processes mobilized and deployed to push them outside the human ocumene.

It is a paradox that was well summarized by Lewis R. Gordon (2008: 87) in this way: 'What should those who live in the polis but are structurally outside of it do if they do not accept their place of being insiders who have been pushed outside'. It is a knotty and perennial question of the historical and discursive formation of a racialized identity born out of denial of the humanity of black people by others. It is a question of the essence and meaning of 'blackism on a world scale' and how it can be understood from a world systems analysis and a decolonial ethical humanist perspective (Ndlovu-Gatsheni 2013a, 2013b). While Ngugi wa Thiong'o (2012: 22) understood 'blackism on a world scale' as a form of cultural reflection of pan-Africanism embracing the negritude movement, in this book it is defined in terms of the experience of being black in a modern world system that emerged in 1492.

The years 1492 and 1497 witnessed two important events that marked the beginning of the unfolding of Euro-America-centric modernity. These were Christopher Columbus's claim to have 'discovered' a 'New World' when he reached the Americas, and Vasco da Gama's successful passage round the Cape of Good Hope while seeking a route to the East Indies. Adam Smith and Karl Marx highlighted the dangers that were contained in these breakthroughs and 'discoveries'. Smith noted that the two events 'were the greatest and most important in the history of mankind: the discovery of America, and the passage to the East Indies by way of the Cape of Good Hope'. He posed the question: 'What benefits, or what misfortune to mankind, may hereafter result from these great events', but concluded that 'no human wisdom can foresee' (Smith 1776). Even though Smith could not be precise on the implications of these 'discoveries' and break-throughs, he foresaw that 'the savage injustice of Europeans [would] render an event, which ought to have been beneficial to all, ruinous and destructive to several of those unfortunate countries' (ibid.).

Karl Marx was more direct on the disastrous implications of the discovery of gold and silver in the Americas and the 'discovery' of the passage to the East Indies. He wrote about how these events led to 'extirpation, enslavement and entombment in the mines. For India it led to its conquest and plunder, and Africa was converted into a preserve for commercial hunting of black skins', concluding that these development 'characterized the rosy dawn of capitalist production' (Marx 1867). The dawn of Euro-North American-centric modernity was accompanied by the invention of 'blackism on a world scale'.

## Blackism on a World Scale

'Blackism on a world scale' as a racial problem arose from how a Euro-North American-centric world as it unfolded in terms of racial profiling and racial hierarchization of the human population resulted in the inhuman act of denying the humanity of other human beings. This denial of the humanity of black people happened in tandem with Euro-North American-centric modernity's drive to colonize space, time, being, knowledge and even nature. This drive resulted in the usurpation of world history by the Euro-North Americans giving birth to such processes as Hellenocentrism (privileging of Greek and Roman civilizations as foundational to all other civilization while neglecting non-European ones), Eurocentrism (making Europe the centre of the world and denigration of the world outside Europe) and Westernization (attempts to remake the whole world in the image of Europe and North America) (Dussel 2011).

The act of denial of black people's humanity is foundational to a plethora of other denials and justifications. These include denial of a dignified space in the modern world as well as the definition of black people as either a problem to be eliminated or a natural resource for cheap labour. Denials were justified on such spurious grounds as black people lack souls, history, writing, civilization, development, democracy, human rights, and ethics. This catalogue of justifications of denials of humanity of non-European people was well summarized by Ramon Grosfoguel:

> We went from the sixteenth-century characterization of a 'people without writing' to the eighteenth and nineteenth-centuries characterization of 'people without history', to the twentieth-century characterization of 'people without development', and more recently, to the early twenty-first century of 'people without democracy'. (Grosfoguel 2007: 214)

This is a perennial historical, philosophical and practical question; it boils down to what it means to be black in the modern world, and has occupied the minds of such scholars as Lewis R. Gordon (1995, 1997, 2000) in the field of black existential philosophy. At the centre of the problem is black people's sense of 'self-image' and 'self-determination', as articulated by Cornell West (1999).

This reality provoked the humanist and celebrated Nigerian novelist Chinua Achebe to remind his Western audience in one of his numerous lectures of the fact that the world was big and that the problem was that some people were failing to comprehend such a simple fact to the extent of wishing they were the only human beings on earth (Achebe in Arana 2002). He challenged his Western audience to grow from wanting the world 'on their own terms' to be inhabited by them, by people like them, and by their friends. Achebe dismissed this thinking as 'a foolish and blind wish' simply because 'diversity is not an abnormality but the very reality of our planet' (ibid.: 505). Achebe was railing against those who wished for a world without others except themselves. His critique was a direct indictment of those who claimed 'being' for themselves while reducing all other people to the realm of 'becoming'.

## The Sins of the Cartesian Subject

The culprit here is what has come to be known as the 'Cartesian Subject'. The modern world that emerged in 1492 was driven

**129**

and ordered by this Cartesian Subject, defined as a rational being endowed with sufficient rationality and scientific knowledge to overcome all obstacles facing humanity. The birth of the Cartesian Subject was revolutionary as it was born out of transcendence of the 'Lacanian void'. Prior to the rise of the Cartesian Subject, a Lacanian void haunted humanity as it was not easy for human beings to define and distinguish themselves from other species. Religion dominated the world by then. The trick as to how to transcend the Lacanian void was offered by Rene Descartes (1968). He identified rational thinking as the defining feature of being human.

Descartes articulated this in terms of 'cogito ergo sum' (I think, therefore I am). Having transcended the Lacanian void, the Cartesian Subject not only assumed some God-like tendencies such as elevating itself above nature and claiming to produce universal knowledge, but also aspired to live in a world without others. This is evident from the way the Cartesian Subject projected itself as the only 'Being' while relegated others to the domain of perpetual 'Becoming'. This thinking manifested itself poignantly during the age of colonial encounters as notions of 'cogito ergo sum' intersected with ideas of 'ergo conquistus' (I conquer, therefore I am) (Maldonado-Torres 2007).

The notions 'Being' for 'them/us', and 'Becoming' for 'others', became articulated in modernist-racial terms and was routinized as natural states of being. Here was born the 'colour line' that was eloquently articulated by William E.B. du Bois as the major problem of the twentieth century. It is a problem that has continued into the twenty-first century. Decolonization has not yet fully managed to decolonize, deimperialize or transform the racially hierarchized, patriarchal, Euro-North-American-centric, Christian-centric, hetero-normative, sexist, capitalist, imperial, colonial and modern world system (Grosfoguel 2007).

## The Perennial Challenge of the Colour Line

This enduring 'colour line' is a product of modernity. Modernity produced a racially hierarchized world system and an imperial global order underpinned by colonialism and capitalism. The modernity referred to here is best understood as 'Euro-North American' modernity to distinguish it from other 'modernities' or 'trans-modernities'. Euro-North American modernity unfolded in terms of the colonization of time (ancient vs. modern), space (mapping of continents, establishment of colonies and modern nation-states), being (racial hierarchization, profiling and racial representation of people), knowledge (appropriation of some, displacement of others, and silencing and subjugating of yet others), and nature (reduction to a natural resource that is open for unlimited exploitation).

Writing about this situation of a racially hierarchized modern world system, the leading philosopher Lewis R. Gordon stated: 'Born from the divide of black and white, it serves as a blueprint of the ongoing division of humankind'. He elaborated that '[t]he color line is also a metaphor that exceeds its own concrete formulation. It is the race line as well as the gender line, the class line, the sexual orientation line, the religious line – in short, the line between "normal" and "abnormal" identities' (Gordon 2000: 63). The subject of the dividing 'line' preoccupied the Portuguese sociologist Boaventura de Sousa Santos to the extent of linking it to the Western 'abyssal thinking'. This is how he understood the genealogy and significance of the 'line':

> Modern Western thinking is an abyssal thinking. It consists of a system of visible and invisible distinctions, the invisible ones being the foundation of the visible ones. The invisible distinctions are established through radical lines that divide social reality into two realms, the realm of 'this side of the line' and the realm of 'the other side of the line'. The division is such that 'the other side of the line' vanishes as reality. Non-existent means not existing in any relevant or comprehensive way of being. Whatever is produced as non-existent is radically excluded because it lies beyond the realm of what the accepted conception of inclusion considers to be its order. What fundamentally characterizes abyssal thinking is thus the impossibility of the co-presence of the two sides of the line. To the extent that it prevails, this side of the line only prevails by exhausting the field of relevant reality. Beyond it, there is only non-existence, invisibility, non-dialectical absence. (Santos 2007: 45–46)

The question of the 'line' has also occupied the celebrated African scholar Valentin Y. Mudimbe in his engagement with the 'invention of Africa' and the 'idea of Africa' as products of the paradigm of difference. In his most recent major work entitled *On African Fault Lines: Mediations on Alterity Politics* (2013), Mudimbe continues to grapple with the broader contemporary issues of ontological lines, disciplinary lines and lines of comprehension, as well as their implications for expressions of the African condition. He delves deeper into critical humanistic reflections on the realities of 'being in the world' where alienation, creativity and ethics of living together coexist paradoxically. His interventions propelled him to deal with epistemological issues informing intellectual articulation of Africa's place in the present economic and cultural global configurations, as well as the ubiquity of paradigms of difference and politics of alterity that continue to haunt the African world in particular and the rest of the world in general (ibid.: 21–23).

One can safely say that the post-1492 Euro-North American-centric modernity that is not only entangled in imperiality and coloniality but is also underpinned by linear and horizontal heterarchies (complex lines) that perpetuate paradigms of difference and discourses of alterity. As articulated by William E.B. Du Bois (1898), the black subject re-emerged from modernity as a problem for the 'Cartesian Subject'. Cartesian subjectivity had been assumed and monopolized by Europeans and North Americans. Black people were excluded from what Nelson Maldonado-Torres (2007) termed the 'human ocumene'. Defining black people as a problem rather than a people with a problem enabled all sorts of abuses, including 'final solutions' (genocide). Colonial genocides were underpinned by epistemicides as part of the broader global imperial designs aimed at creating 'a world without others'.

The Cartesian Subject arrogated to itself ontological density while doubting the humanity of others. Thus modern subjecthood was claimed by Europeans as they reconstructed and positioned themselves as the 'master subject' race. They claimed to be the paragons of rationality and science. The long-term consequences of this thinking on Western notions of subjectivity and identity were well summarized by Patrick Chabal in these revealing words:

> So, starting at the beginning, we in the West think of ourselves as self-standing, autonomous and rational individuals, who have chosen the ways in which we live socially together. We see such a way of being as the logical outcome of the development of society since the Enlightenment and the rise of the scientific understanding of the world, which have led to the Industrial Revolution and the production of the technology on which our everyday lives depend. We consider the protection of individual human rights as the pinnacle of a civilized way of living, in which we value each other as persons and seek to protect both our individuality and our personality from undue interference from others or from the state. Therefore we view our conception of the human being and our arrangements for living in society both as the most progressive and as being possessed of the greatest potential for individual advancement. As we see it, it is because of the way we have managed to liberate and protect the individual that we make it possible for each person to seek the best for him/herself. ...
>
> [B]ut the upshot of this view we have of ourselves inevitably generates a sense of Western superiority. We don't like to gloat or to make it too obvious, but deep down we do believe that our social, political and economic arrangements are not just the best in the history of mankind but also, and this is crucial, the best in the present historical circumstances. ...
>
> I am less interested here in debating whether this Western economic and political dispensation is effectively the best than in looking at the consequences of such assumptions for the way in which we see ourselves and look upon others. For it is indeed the case that such a vision of our 'progress' implies a sense of distinction that puts distance between us and others. (Chabal 2012: 119–22)

This Western conception of themselves, of their institutions, values and trajectories crystallized at a time when they expanded beyond their locations into other parts of the world through what became known as 'voyages of discovery'. These processes culminated in the birth of an identity of a people called 'blacks'. Prior to the enslavement of African people an identity called 'black' did not exist. It was produced by the manifestations of the 'darker side' of modernity that enabled such inimical processes as the slave trade, imperialism, colonialism, apartheid and neo-colonialism.

As noted by Arturo Escobar, these processes cascading from the 'dark side' of modernity combined to create what became known as the Third World. The epistemic sites of Latin America, the Caribbean, Asia and Africa constitute the core of the Third World, which in recent years has come to be described as the Developing World or the Global South – terms that seek to hide coloniality. Today, these places are suffering from global coloniality, a racial power structure in place since conquest.

Blackism on a world scale is now a creature of global coloniality sustained by a world system that is resistant to decolonization and deimperialization. The consciousness of 'being black' emerged inside those notorious vessels that transported African people as slaves. The 'middle passage' was not only a terrain of suffering and death; it was also a nursery for black consciousness formation. This is a point well articulated by C.L.R. James: 'Contrary to the lies that have been spread so pertinaciously about Negro docility, the revolts at the port of embarkation and on board were incessant, so that the slaves had to be chained, right hand to right leg, left hand to left leg, and attached in rows to long iron bars' (James 1963: 8). Blackness as an identity consolidated itself within the confines of the plantations. This is why the plantation became not only a site of racial oppression, brutality and naked exploitation of labour without any payment, but also a site of struggles and resistance within which blackism as consciousness matured. Blackism unfolded as an anti-racist discourse. It matured into pan-Africanism and nationalism. It delivered decolonization.

But blackism remains a state of being and a form of subjectivity that was and is mostly articulated in negative terms. Beginning with early harbingers of coloniality like Christopher Columbus, those people with black and brown skins were considered not to be human enough. First, the colonialists questioned whether such people had religion. Second, the colonialists doubted whether such people had souls. Third, colonialists denied that black people had history. Fourth, colonialists doubted whether black people had any civilization. This imperial attitude and scepticism continued into the twentieth and twenty-first centuries, whereby colonialists described black people as lacking development, lacking democracy and lacking human rights. This point is well articulated by Ramon Grosfoguel:

> This epistemic strategy has been crucial for Western global designs. By hiding the location of the subject of enunciation, European/Euro-American colonial expansion and domination was able to construct a hierarchy of superior and inferior knowledge and, thus, of superior and inferior people around the world. (Grosfoguel 2007: 214)

Within the discursive terrain of modernity, imperiality and coloniality, the only people with ontological density were those with white skins. Ideally, these people wanted to live in a world without others as they considered themselves to be the only authentic human beings. Africans were first approached as items of trade. They were indeed violently captured and traded as slaves. If not directly traded as commodities, they were dispossessed and redefined as peasants and sources of cheap labour without any sense of property ownership. This constituted the global division of labour, which became the central leitmotif of the global capitalist system. Since 1492, those locales outside Europe and North America that happened to fall victim to colonization have not recovered from peripherization, subalternization and pauperization.

The Mandela phenomenon could not escape engaging with and articulating the foundations of the paradigm of difference and the essence of the discourse of alterity as this articulated the reality of being black within a modern world order that is racially hierarchized, Western-centric, Christian-centric, hetero-normative, patriarchal and capitalist. Within this world order blackness is being treated with utmost disdain. Black people are not free to travel across the world. Visa regimes are used throughout the world to exclude mainly Africans from those places designated as zones of peace and prosperity.

Policies of reconciliation pronounced at the end of direct colonialism have not succeeded in resolving the native–settler Manichean structure created by Euro-North American-centric modernity/imperiality/coloniality. This entangled Manichean structure of power has continued to provoke endless wars across the human globe, including terrorism. This has seen decolonial humanists actively trying to come up with creative and innovative ways of transcending the paradigm of war and transform the world into a new pluriversal one in which race is not the organizing principle. Mandela was a frontline cadre

## The Paradigm of Peace and Restorative Justice

The long-standing challenge that has faced advocates of decolonial humanism has been how to transcend the paradigm of war that has been naturalized in Western philosophical thought. Decolonial humanists of which Mandela was a leading light, building on a rich tradition traceable to CLR James, William EB Du Bois, Aime Cesaire, Frantz Fanon, Thomas Sankara, Stephen Bantu Biko, Julius Nyerere and many others, have challenged the idea of war as natural. They have challenged the idea of the inherent evilness of human beings. They have refused to embrace race as the organizing principle of modern life. They have sought to revive the humanist spirit that was destroyed by the slave trade, imperialism, colonialism and apartheid. They have sought to appeal to the natural goodness of human beings. They have questioned the value of justice that is predicated on an eye for an eye. They have embraced ubuntu as the centrepiece of a new civilizational project aimed at creating a new humanism and a pluriversal world.

Consequently, decolonial humanism has been very critical of the current ways of dealing with situations of conflict, war and mass violence through the use of the courts to achieve criminal justice. Mandela was a leading advocate of new paradigm shifts in the mediation and resolution of conflicts, particularly those involving mass violence. He strongly believed in working towards winning the enemy over and in the process transforming that enemy into an adversary open to dialogue and negotiations. In the second instance, Mandela emphasized the strategy of working with the adversary to build peace collectively, having first convinced the former enemy of the futility of engaging in war and violence, and opening his eyes to the collective peace dividend.

This approach in searching for peace has caught the eye of the leading African scholar Mahmood Mamdani, who has studied conflicts, wars and mass violence including genocide in such places as South Africa, Uganda, Rwanda, the Democratic Republic of Congo and Sudan, and also of the former president of South Africa, Thabo Mbeki, who has been a mediator and negotiator in various conflicts including in South Africa, Zimbabwe, Cote D'Ivoire and Sudan. The consensus they seem to have reached is that 'courts can't end civil wars' (Mbeki and Mamdani 2014). The use of courts as a mediator and solution to crimes of mass violence was used at the end of the Second World War in what became known as the Nuremberg Trials involving those members of Nazi Germany who had been selected for individual criminalization and punishment as perpetrators of violence.

Mbeki and Mamdani have posited that '[s]ince the end of the Cold War, the world has looked to the Nuremberg Trials as a model for closure in the wake of extreme violence'. They further argued that '[t]he International Criminal Court is built on the model of Nuremberg' (Mbeki and Mamdani 2014). They seem to favour the CODESA template of justice over the Nuremberg one because the former conceived the apartheid-generated conflict as a political conflict and the mass violence it generated as political violence, and then suggested that the resolution was a political settlement born out of political justice in which survivors endeavour to live together again as citizens.

What Mbeki and Mamdani are critiquing is the value of criminalizing political conflicts, in the process trying to create a demarcation between victims and perpetrators. They argue in the Mandela-style that this Nuremberg tradition of privileging trials has failed to heal nations emerging from war and mass violence. They motivate for a political approach 'driven by a firm conviction that there can be no winners and no losers, only survivors', because '[i]n civil wars, no one is wholly innocent and no one is wholly guilty' (Mbeki and Mamdani 2014).

This approach has the potential to resolve the circle that Mamdani (2001b) aptly summarized as 'When Victims Become Killers', with specific reference to the Rwandan Genocide of 1994. This is the best way to conclude this book on Mandela.

He was very sensitive to the trap of making today's victims the killers of tomorrow. He wisely pushed for a political solution rather than a criminal solution to the apartheid-generated conflict. What he reaped at the end was one of the celebrated constitutions and a functioning democracy, albeit still within the context of a world system that is resistant to decolonization and a global order that is opposed to deimperialization.

## Mandela's Foreign Policy and the Vision of a Peaceful World

Mandela's foreign policy was grounded on deep decolonial humanism. Mandela articulated his ideas for a new world in 1993 in an article that was published by the influential *Foreign Affairs* journal. In this article Mandela spelt out six pillars of South Africa's envisaged foreign policy:

(1) That issues of human rights are central to international relations, and an understanding that they extend beyond the political, embracing the economic, social and environmental;
(2) That just and lasting solutions to the problems of humankind can only come through the promotion of democracy worldwide;
(3) That considerations of justice and respect for international law should guide the relations between nations;
(4) That peace is the goal that all nations should strive for, and where this breaks down, internationally agreed and non-violent mechanisms, including effective arms control, must be employed;
(5) That the concerns and interests of the continent of Africa should be reflected in our foreign policy choices; and
(6) That economic development depends on growing regional and international economic cooperation in an interdependent world. (Mandela 1993: 2)

As a decolonial humanist and an advocate of the paradigm of peace and justice, Mandela put protection of human rights and promotion of democracy at the centre of his articulation of South African foreign policy. This is how he put it:

Because the world is a more dangerous place, the international community dare not relinquish its commitment to human rights. The appeal also has a special significance for South Africa. The anti-apartheid campaign was the most important human rights crusade of post-World War II. Its success was a demonstration, in my opinion, of the oneness of our common humanity: in these troubled times, its passion should not be lost. Consequently, South Africa will not be indifferent to the rights of others. Human rights will be the light that guides our foreign affairs. Only true democracy can guarantee rights. (Mandela 1993: 3)

Mandela was aware of the problem of asymmetrical global power relations and the need for a restructuring and democratization of this configuration of power that led the United Nations to be dominated by a group of a few powerful nations. He was also aware that this asymmetrical global power structure has been sustained by a paradigm of war that enabled the accumulation of arms of mass destruction; hence he called for a 'commitment to a general and complete disarmament under effective international law' (Mandela 1993: 5).

Like all decolonial humanists, Mandela also emphasized the need to bridge the gap between the rich and the poor across the world: 'If there is to be global harmony, the international community will have to discover mechanisms to bridge the divide between its rich and its poor' (Mandela 1993: 3). Mandela also raised concerns about a world that was engulfed by narrow nationalism that was Balkanizing states and invoking 'ancient and long-dormant animosities'. All these were clear indications of a world that Mandela envisioned.

James Barber (2004) wrote about 'Mandela's World' in his analysis of the international dimensions of the South African political revolution between 1990 and 1999. He captured well the complexities of 'Mandela's World' when he wrote that post-apartheid South Africa emerged in a changed and uncertain world, marked by contradictory tendencies and impulses of, on the one hand, 'the grim prospect of a retribalization of large swaths of humankind by war and bloodshed', and on the other, 'a busy portrait of onrushing economic, technological and ecological forces that demand integration and uniformity' (ibid.: 5; Barber 2005). Parochial nationalism, sometimes known as xenophobia, produced the Rwandan Genocide during the same time that South

Africa was celebrating the demise of administrative apartheid. The universal impulse was mainly manifest in the globalization of capitalist markets trampling national and continental borders in search of consumers and profits.

Because the modern world system was still resistant to decolonization and the global orders it produced epochally were equally resistant to deimperialization, Mandela's attempts to implement a human rights oriented foreign policy earned him a reputation for being an idealist, but he was frustrated and humiliated in many instances. Habib wrote:

> In the initial years under Mandela, South Africa's foreign policy took on a naive, almost crusading human rights quality, that reached its zenith when Mandela called for opposition to Nigeria's Sani Abacha at the Conference of Commonwealth Heads of Government in 1995 for the hanging of Ken Saro-Wiwa and his compatriots, and in 1997 when Mandela negotiated with Mobutu Sese Seko on a South African navy ship off the coast of the Democratic Republic of Congo. The low point came shortly thereafter, as it became clear that South Africa's attempts to isolate Nigeria had failed. (Habib 2013: 176)

Mandela's naivety was that he tried practically to implement his human rights oriented foreign policy in a world that was struck in a paradigm of war and retributive justice, including use of the death penalty to punish political opponents. The naivety of Mandela was that once more he was ahead of his time. He strongly believed in a pluriversal world in which political differences, ethnic differences, racial differences and gender differences were to be tolerated across the human globe. For this strong belief he was deemed to be a naive idealist. Mandela's commitment to the promotion of what Barber (2005: 1082) terms 'good causes' left him with egg on his face simply because the world was still struck in pursuit of 'bad causes'.

On the Nigerian case the notorious military dictator Sani Abacha had executed ten Ogoni activists led by the novelist and human rights activist Ken Saro-Wiwa. The humanist Mandela out of all world leaders saw this as an infringement of human rights. He then tried to mobilize the world to diplomatically isolate Nigeria and even impose sanctions so as to send a strong message of condemnation of the violation of human rights. He went further and recalled the South African High Commissioner to Nigeria as part of protesting Abacha's human rights violations. As detailed by Barber:

His efforts produced nothing. The West continued to buy oil, and the African states had no appetite for confrontation. They saw Nigeria not as an abuser of human rights, but a continental leader, which had supported other liberation struggles and was a major contributor to the OAU. They accused Mandela of breaking African unity. Indignantly, Liberia claimed that the 'campaign against Nigeria is very shocking', and called on others 'not to allow South Africa to be used in undermining of African solidarity'. The Nigerians themselves described Mandela's attitude as 'horrific and terrible', and spoke of South Africa as 'a white state with a black head'. Even at home Mandela gained little support. After it was pointed out that Nigeria had given substantial financial support to the ANC's electoral chest, the government started back-pedalling. Mbeki told parliament that South Africa must act not alone but in concert. (Barber 2005: 1084)

Was Mandela wrong in taking a stand against human rights violations in Nigeria? No, he was not. The world was wrong to condone such a violation of human rights. Just like in the 1960s when Mandela was ahead of the world in being prepared to die for democracy and human rights, in the 1990s he was again ahead of other leaders in his commitment to the protection of human rights and the promotion of democracy across the world. Whatever criticisms have been levelled against him for promoting a paradigm of peace, for advocating reconciliation and the protection of human rights, and for calling for genuine democracy, Mandela left a dignified legacy from which to continue the decolonial humanist struggle. He is indeed a 'worthy ancestor' who will live forever in our minds. True to his principles, he actively played his role in mediating conflicts in countries such as Burundi, and openly condemned the United States of America and its allies for invading Iraq. He even offered to go to Iraq to act as a human shield to protect the victims of American imperialist wars that were legitimized through the noble discourses of the 'responsibility to protect' (R2P) and the crusade to export democracy and human rights through violent regime changes in the Global South.

At a broader level, the Mandela phenomenon speaks to the challenges of shifting from the paradigm of difference and war that created the conflictual 'us' and 'them' ways of relationality to the new decolonial politics of re-creating and re-inventing human relations around the politics of the common. At the centre of this politics of life has always been the challenge of learning to live and share the planet peacefully. Being 'humans' is that which we share and from which we must build a politics of rehabilitation of the human. At the centre of the rehabilitation of the human is the elusive 'us' as a horizon that has to be created and reached. Mandela was a consistent theorist of 'us' as a horizon. It is clear that he imagined the 'us' as multiplicity. Mandela worked hard to escape what Fanon termed the law of repetition that reproduced the paradigm of war and politics of alterity rather than a paradigm of peace, new humanism and pluriversality. While some can say that Mandela did not succeed in setting afoot a new humanism, there is no doubt that a blueprint was flagged for the present generation to implement or betray.

# References

Adebajo. A. 2010. *The Curse of Berlin: Africa after the Cold War.* Scottsville: University of KwaZulu-Natal Press.

Ahluwalia, P. 2001. *Politics and Post-Colonial Theory: African Inflections.* London and New York: Routledge.

———. 2003. 'The Struggle for African Identity: Thabo Mbeki's African Renaissance', in A. Zegeye and R.L. Harris (eds), *Media, Identity and the Public Sphere in Post-Apartheid South Africa.* Leiden and Boston, MA: Brill, pp. 27–39.

Ake, C. 1979. *Social Science as Imperialism: The Theory of Political Development.* Ibadan, Nigeria: University of Ibadan Press.

Amin, S. 2009. *Eurocentrism: Modernity, Religion, and Democracy: A Critique of Eurocentrism and Culturalism.* Second Edition. Translated by Russell Moore and James Membrez. New York: Monthly Review Press.

Arana, R.V. 2002. 'The Epic Imagination: A Conversation with Chinua Achebe at Annandale-on-Hudson, October 31, 1998', *Callaloo* 24(2) (Spring): 505–26.

Barber, J. 2004. *Mandela's World: The International Dimensions of South Africa's Political Revolution, 1990–99.* Oxford: James Currey; Cape Town: David Philip; Athens: Ohio University Press.

———. 2005. 'The New South Africa's Foreign Policy: Principles and Practice', *International Affairs* 81(5): 1079–96.

Barnard, R. 2014. 'Introduction', in R. Barnard (ed.), *The Cambridge Companion to Nelson Mandela.* Cambridge: Cambridge University Press, pp. 1–45.

Benson, M. 1994. *Nelson Mandela: The Man and the Movement.* Hamondsworth: Penguin.

References

Beresford, A. 2014. 'Nelson Mandela and the Politics of South Africa's Unfinished Liberation', *Review of African Political Economy*: 1–9.

Bhabha, H. 1994. *The Location of Culture*. London: Routledge.

Blair, D. 2002. *Degrees in Violence: Robert Mugabe and the Struggle for Power in Zimbabwe*. New York: Continuum International Publishing Ltd.

Blaut, J.M. 1993. *The Colonizer's Model of the World: Geographical Diffusionism and Eurocentric History*. New York and London: The Guilford Press.

Boehmer, E. 2008. *Nelson Mandela: A Very Short Introduction*. Oxford: Oxford University Press.

Bonner, P. 2014. 'The Antinomies of Nelson Mandela', in R. Barnard (ed.), *The Cambridge Companion to Nelson Mandela*. Cambridge: Cambridge University Press, pp. 29–49.

Bulger, P. 2013. 'Nelson Mandela: An Obituary'. In http://www.bdlive.co.za/opnion/2013/12/06/nelson-mandela-an-obituary?service=print (accessed 9 December 2013).

Campbell, H. 2013. 'Ubuntu and the Emancipation of Human Everywhere: Mandela and the African Liberation Struggle'. *Counterpunch*. http://www.counterpunch.org/2013/12/12/mandela-and-the-african-liberation-struggle/print (Accessed 28/02/2014)

Campbell, J. 1949. *The Hero with a Thousand Faces*. New York: Pantheon Books.

Campbell, K.E. 2012. 'Playing or Proving the Enemy? Mandela's Rhetorical Test', *African Journal of Rhetoric* 4: 48–66.

Carlin, J. 2006. *Playing the Enemy: Nelson Mandela and the Game that Made a Nation*. New York: Penguin Books.

Casimir, J. 2011. 'Haiti's Need for A Great South', *The Global South* 5(1) (Spring): 14–36.

Catholic Commission for Justice and Peace (CCJP) and Legal Resources Foundation Report. 1997. 'Breaking the Silence: A Report on the Disturbances in Matebeleland and the Midlands, 1980–1988'. Harare.

Cesaire, A. 1955. *Discourse on Colonialism*. Translated by Joan Pinkham. New York: Monthly Review Press.

Chabal, P. 2012. *The End of Conceit*. London and New York: Zed Books.

Chinweizu. 1975. *The West and the Rest of Us: White Predators, Black Slavers and the African Elite*. Lagos: Pero Press / New York: Random House.

———. 1987. *Decolonizing the African Mind*. Lagos: Pero Press.

————. 2008. 'What is Ubuntology?', *Guardian*, 27 January.

Cugoano, A.Q. (1789) 1999. *Thoughts on the Evils of Slavery and Other Writings*. New York: Penguin Books.

Darwin, C. (1879) 2011. *The Origins of Species*. London: Harper Press.

Descartes, R. 1968. *Discourse on Method and the Meditations: Translated with an Introduction by F.E. Sutcliffe*. New York: Penguin Books.

————. 2013. *Discours de la Methode*. Cambridge: Cambridge University Press.

Du Bois, W.E.B. 1898. 'The Study of the Negro Problem', *Annals of the American Academy of Political and Social Science* XI (January): 1–23.

————. 1903. *The Souls of Black Folk*. New York : Dover Publications, Inc.

————. 1965. *The World and Africa: An Inquiry into the Part which Africa has Played in World History*. New York: International Publishers.

Dussel, E. 1989. *Philosophy of Liberation*. New York: Orbis.

————. 2008. *Twenty Theses on Politics*. Translated by George Ciccariello-Maher. Durham, NC and London: Duke University Press.

————. 2011. *Politics of Liberation: A Critical World History*. Translated by Thia Cooper. London: SMC Press.

Ellis, S. 2011. 'Mandela, Communism and South Africa.' in *openDemocracy* available at http://www.opendemocracy.net (accessed 4 May 2014).

————. 2013. *External Mission: The ANC in Exile*. Johannesburg and Cape Town: Jonathan Ball Publishers.

Ellis, S., and T. Sechaba. 1992. *Comrades Against Apartheid: The ANC and the South Africa Communist Party in Exile*. Bloomington: Indiana University Press.

Eze, E.C. 2001. *Achieving Our Humanity: The Idea of the Postracial Future*. New York and London: Routledge.

Falola, T. 2001. *Nationalism and African Intellectuals*. Rochester: University of Rochester Press.

————. (ed.). 2004. *Mandela: Tributes to a Global Icon*. Durham, NC: Carolina Academic Press.Fanon, F. 1968. *The Wretched of the Earth*. New York: Grove Press.

Firmin, J.-A. 2002. *The Equality of the Human Races*. Campaign: University of Illinois Press.

Freire, P. 1970. *The Pedagogy of the Oppressed.* New York and London: Continuum.

Goody, J. 2006. *The Theft of History.* Cambridge: Cambridge University Press.

Gordon, L.R. 1995. *Bad Faith and Anti-black Racism.* Atlantic Highlands, NJ: Humanities Press.

———. 1997. *Her Majesty's Other Children: Sketches of Racism from a Neocolonial Age.* Lenham: Rowan & Littlefield.

———. 2000. *Existentia Africana: Understanding Africana Existential Thought.* New York: Routledge.

———. 2008. *An Introduction to African Philosophy.* Cambridge: Cambridge University Press.

Government of the Republic of South Africa. 1994. White Paper on Reconstruction and Development. Pretoria: Government Gazette 353, 23 November.

Grosfoguel, R. 2007. 'The Epistemic Decolonial Turn: Beyond Political-Economy Paradigms', *Cultural Studies* 2(2/3) (March/May): 211–336.

———. 2011. 'Decolonizing Post-Colonial Studies and the Paradigms of Political-Economy: Transmodernity, Decolonial Thinking, and Global Coloniality', *Transmodernity: Journal of Peripheral Cultural Production of the Luso-Hispanic World* 1(1): 1–39.

———. 2013. 'The Structure of Knowledge in Westernized Universities: Epistemic Racism/Sexism and the Four Genocides/Epistemicides of the Long 16th Century', *Human Architecture: Journal of the Sociology of Self-Knowledge* XI(1) (Fall): 73–90.

Habib, A. 2013. *South Africa's Suspended Revolution: Hopes and Prospects.* Johannesburg: Wits University Press.

Halisi, C.R.D. 1999. *Black Political Thought in the Making of South African Democracy.* Bloomington and Indianapolis: Indiana University Press.

Hart, G. 2013. *Rethinking the South African Crisis: Nationalism, Populism, Hegemony.* Scottsville: University of KwaZulu-Natal.

Hobbes, T. 1958. *Leviathan-Part I and II.* New York: Macmillan Publishing Company.

Hyslop, J. 2014. 'Mandela on War', in R. Barnard (ed.), *The Cambridge Companion to Nelson Mandela.* Cambridge: Cambridge University Press, pp. 162–81.

James, C.L.R. 1963. *The Black Jacobins: Toussaint L'Ouverture and the San Domingo Revolution*. Second Edition, Revised. New York: Vintage Books.

Joffe, J. 2007. *The State vs. Nelson Mandela*. Oxford: Oneworld.

Kant, I. 1996. 'An Answer to the Question: What is Enlightenment?', in J. Schmidt (ed.), *What is Enlightenment?: Eighteenth-Century Answers and Twentieth-Century Questions*. Berkeley, Los Angeles: University of California Press.

Kathrada, A. 2011. 'Reconciliation and Nation-Building: The Mandela Way' in *The Hindu*, July 18, pp. 1–2.

Kaunda, K., and C.M. Morris. 1966. *A Humanist in Africa: Letters to Colin M. Morris from Kenneth D. Kaunda, President of Zambia*. New York: Abingdon Press.

Levander, C., and W. Mignolo. 2011. 'Introduction: The Global South and World Dis/order', *The Global South* 5(1) (Spring): 1–11.

Lodge, T. 2006. *Mandela: A Critical Life*. Oxford: Oxford University Press.

Luthuli, A.J. 1961. 'Nobel Peace Prize Acceptance Speech', 11 December. http://www.anc.org.za/show.php?id=4296 (accessed 6 May 2014).

Magubane, B.M. 2007. *Race and the Construction of the Dispensable Other*. Pretoria: University of South Africa Press.

Magubane, B., et al. 2004. 'The Turn to Armed Struggle', in *The Road to Democracy in South Africa: Volume 1 (1960–1970)*. Pretoria: UNISA Press, pp. 49–133.

Maldonado-Torres, N. 2004. 'The Topography of Being and the Geopolitics of Knowledge: Modernity, Empire, Coloniality', *City* 8(1) (April): 29–56.

———. 2007. 'On Coloniality of Being: Contributions to the Development of a Concept', *Cultural Studies* 21(2/3) (March/May): 240–70.

———. 2008a. 'Lewis Gordon: Philosopher of the Human', *CLR James Journal* 14(1): 103–37.

———. 2008b. *Against War: View from the Underside of Modernity*. Durham, NC: Duke University Press.

Malema, J. 2014. 'EFF Inspired by the Real Nelson Mandela'. *City Press*, 22 April.

Mamdani, M. 1991. 'Social Movements and Constitutionalism in the African Context', in I.G. Shivji (ed.), *State and Constitutionalism:*

*An African Debate on Democracy*. Harare: SAPES Books, pp. 236–37.

——. 1996. *Citizen and Subject: Contemporary Africa and the Legacy of Late Colonialism*. Princeton, NJ: Princeton University Press.

——. 1998. 'When Does a Settler Become a Native? Reflections on the Roots of Citizenship in Equatorial and South Africa'. Inaugural Lecture, University of Cape Town.

——. 2001a. 'When Does a Settler Become a Native? Citizenship and Identity in a Settler Society'. *Pretext: Literary and Cultural Studies* 10(1) (July): 63–89.

——. 2001b. *When Victims Become Killers: Colonialism, Nativism, and the Genocide in Rwanda*. Kampala: Fountain Publishers.

——. 2002. 'Amnesty or Impunity? A Preliminary Critique of the Report of the Truth and Reconciliation Commission of South Africa (TRC)', *Diacritics* 32(3) (Fall/Winter): 33–59.

——. 2009. *Saviours and Survivors: Darfur, Politics and the War on Terror*. Cape Town: Human Science Research Council Press.

——. 2010. 'Lessons of Nuremberg and CODESA: Where Do We Go From Here?' Unpublished paper presented at the 2010 Africa Memorial Day Talk, University of the Free State, 14 July.

——. 2013a. 'Beyond Nuremberg: The Historical Significance of the Post-Apartheid Transition in South Africa'. Unpublished 2013 Annual Inaugural Lecture, delivered at Mapungubwe Institute for Strategic Reflection, University of Witwatersrand, 18 March.

——. 2013b. 'The Logic of Nuremberg', *London Review of Books* (7 November): 33–34.

——. 2013c. *Define and Rule: Native as Political Identity*. Johannesburg: Wits University Press.

Mandela, N. 1993. 'South Africa's Future Foreign Policy', *Foreign Affairs* 75(5), available at http://www.anc.org.za/show.php?id=4113 (accessed 22 June 2014).

——. 1994. *Long Walk to Freedom: The Autobiography of Nelson Mandela*. London: Little, Brown and Company.

——. 2010. *Conversations With Myself*. New York: Farr, Straus and Giroux.

Mangcu, X. (ed.). 2011. *Becoming Worthy Ancestors: Archive, Public Deliberation and Identity in South Africa*. Johannesburg: Wits University Press.

Marx, K. (1867) 1976. *Capital: Volume 1*. London: New Left Books.

Maylam, P. 2005. *The Cult of Rhodes: Remembering an Imperialist in Africa*. Cape Town: David Philip.

————. 2009. 'Archetypal Hero or Living Saint? The Veneration of Nelson Mandela', *Historia* 54(2): 21–36.

Mbeki, T. 1996. 'Speech Delivered on the Occasion of the Adoption of Constitutional Assembly of the Republic of South Africa Constitutional Bill'. Cape Town, South Africa.

Mbeki, T., and M. Mamdani. 2014. 'Courts Can't End Civil Wars', *New York Times*, 5 February.Mbembe, A. 2001. *On the Postcolony*. Berkeley: University of California Press.

————. 2013. 'Frantz Fanon's Oeuvres: A Metamorphic Thought', *Journal of Contemporary African Art* 32 (Spring): 8–17.

Mda, Z. 2013. 'Nelson Mandela: Neither Sell-Out Nor Saint'. *The Guardian*, 6 December.

Meer, F. 1988. *Higher Than Hope: Rolihlahla We Love You: Nelson Mandela's Biography on his 70th Birthday*. Johannesburg: Skotaville Publishers.

Mendieta, E. 2008. 'Foreword. The Liberation of Politics: Alterity, Solidarity, Liberation', in E. Dussel, *Twenty Theses on Politics*. Translated by George Ciccariello-Maher. Durham, NC and London: Duke University Press, pp. vii–xiii.

Meredith, M. 1997. *Nelson Mandela: A Biography*. London: Penguin.

Mignolo, W.D. 1995. *The Darker Side of Renaissance: Literacy, Territory, and Colonization*. Ann Arbor: University of Michigan Press.

————. 2000. *Local Histories/Global Designs: Coloniality, Subaltern Knowledges, and Border Thinking*. Princeton, NJ: Princeton University Press.

————. 2011. *The Darker Side of Western Modernity: Global Futures, Decolonial Options*. Durham, NC and London: Duke University Press.

Mkandawire, T. 2013. 'For my Generation, the Death of Mandela Marks the End of Africa's Liberation'. http://blogs.lse.ac.uk/africaatlse/2013/12/06/for-my-generation-the-death-of-mandela-mar... (accessed 9 December 2013)

Mngxitama, A. 2008. 'Mandela as South Africa's Metaphor'. http://pambazuka.org/en/category/features/49491 (accessed 10 April 2014).

Modisane, C. 2014. 'How Mandela's ANC Sold Out the Economic Struggle'. Available at http://ewn.co.za/2014/04/24/Opnion-How-Mandelas-ANC-sold-out-the-economic-struggle (accessed 30 April 2014).

More, P.M. (no date). 'The Transformative Power of Lewis Gordon's Africana Philosophy in Mandela's House'. Unpublished draft paper.

Mudimbe, V.Y. 2013. *On African Fault Lines: Meditations on Alterity Politics*. Scottsville: University of KwaZulu-Natal Press.

Mugabe, R.G. 2001. *Inside the Third Chimurenga*. Harare: Department of Information and Publicity.

Munro, B. 2014. 'Nelson, Winnie, and the Politics of Gender', in R. Barnard (ed.), *The Cambridge Companion to Nelson Mandela*. Cambridge: Cambridge University Press, pp. 92–112.

Muzondidya, J. 2010. 'The Zimbabwean Crisis and the Unresolved Conundrum of Race in Post-Colonial Period', *Journal of Developing Societies* 28(1): 5–38.

Ndlovu, S.M. 2010. 'The African National Congress and Negotiations', in *The Road to Democracy in South Africa: Volume 4 (1980–1990) Part 1*. Pretoria: UNISA Press, pp. 63–131.

―――. 2013. 'The ANC, CODESA, Substantive Negotiation and the Road to the First Democratic Elections', in *The Road to Democracy in South Africa: Volume 6 (1990–1996) Part 2*. Pretoria: UNISA Press, pp. 723–94.

Ndlovu-Gatsheni, S.J. 2009a. 'Africa for Africans or "Natives" Only? New Nationalism and Nativism in Zimbabwe and South Africa', *Afrika Spectrum* 1: 61–78.

―――. 2009b. 'Making Sense of Mugabeism in Local and Global Politics: "So Blair Keep Your England and Let Me Keep My Zimbabwe"', *Third World Quarterly* 30(6): 1139–58.

―――. 2012a. 'Beyond the Equator There Are No Sins: Coloniality of Being and Violence in Africa,' *Journal of Developing Societies*, 28(4), (2012): 419-440.

―――. 2012b. 'Rethinking Chimurenga and Gukurahundi in Zimbabwe: A Critique of Partisan National History', *African Studies Review* 55(3) (December): 1–26.

―――. 2013a. 'The Entrapment of Africa within the Global Colonial Matrices of Power: Eurocentrism, Coloniality, and Deimperialization in the Twenty-first Century,' *Journal of Developing Societies*, 29(4), pp. 331-353.

―――. 2013b. *Coloniality of Power in Postcolonial Africa: Myths of Decolonization*. Dakar: CODESRIA Book Series.

―――. 2013c. *Empire, Global Coloniality and African Subjectivity*. New York and Oxford: Berghahn Books.

Netshitenzhe, J. 2012. 'Second Keynote Address: A Continuing Search for Identity: Carrying the Burden of History', in A. Lissoni et al. (eds), *One Hundred Years of the ANC: Debating Liberation Histories Today*. Johannesburg: Wits University Press, pp. 13–27.

Newton-King, S. 1981. 'The Rebellion of the Khoi in Graafff-Reinet, 1799–1803', in S. Newton-King and V.C. Malherbe (eds), *The Khoikhoi Rebellion in the Eastern Cape, 1799–1803*. Cape Town: Centre for African Studies, University of Cape Town, pp. 13–37.

Ngugi wa Thiong'o. 1986. *Decolonizing the Mind: The Politics of Language in African Literature*. Nairobi: Heinemann Publishing Ltd.

———. 1993. *Moving the Centre: The Struggle for Cultural Freedoms*. London and Oxford: James Currey.

———. 2009. *Re-membering Africa*. Nairobi: East African Educational Publishers Ltd.

———. 2012. *Globalectics: Theory and the Politics of Knowing*. New York: Columbia University Press.Ngwane, Z. 2014. 'Mandela and Tradition', in R. Barnard (ed.), *The Cambridge Companion to Nelson Mandela*. Cambridge: Cambridge University Press, pp. 115–33.

Nietzsche, F. (1909) 1990. *Beyond Good and Evil*. New York: Penguin.

———. 1968. *The Will to Power*. New York: Vintage.

Nkrumah, K. (1964). *Conscienscism: Philosophy and Ideology for Decolonization*. London: Heinemann

Nuttall, S., and A. Mbembe. 2014. 'Mandela's Mortality', in R. Barnard (ed.), *The Cambridge Companion to Nelson Mandela*. Cambridge: Cambridge University Press, pp. 267–89.

Nyerere, J.K. 1968. *Freedom and Socialism*. New York: Oxford University Press.

Ottaway, S. 1993. *Chained Together: Mandela, de Klerk, and the Struggle to Remake South Africa*. Brunswick: Rutgers University Press.

Peet, R. 2002. 'Ideology, Discourse, and the Geography of Hegemony: From Socialist to Neoliberal Development in Post-apartheid South Africa', *Antipode* 34(1): 54–84.

Pere, G. le. 2014. 'The Past as Prologue: Deconstructing South Africa's Liberation History: Review of *External Mission: The ANC in Exile, 1960–1999* by Stephen Ellis', *Africa Review of Books* 10(1): 4–6.

Pillay, S. 2009. 'Conclusion', in C.L. Sriram and S. Pillay (eds), *Peace versus Justice? The Dilemma of Transitional Justice in Africa*. Pietermaritzburg: University of KwaZulu-Natal Press, pp. 347–57.

Preez Bezdrop, A.M. du. 2003. *Winnie Mandela: A Life*. Cape Town: Zebra Press.

Quijano, A. 2000. 'Coloniality of Power, Eurocentrism, and Latin America', *Nepantla: Views from the South* 1(3): 533–79.

———. 2007. 'Coloniality and Modernity/Rationality', *Cultural Studies* 21(2/3) (March/May): 168–78.

Rabaka, R. 2010. *African Critical Theory: Reconstructing the Black Radical Tradition, from W. E.B. and C.L.R. James to Frantz Fanon and Amilcar Cabral*. Lenham, MD and Boulder, CO: Lexington Books.

Ramphela, M. 2008. *Laying Ghosts to Rest: Dilemmas of the Transformation in South Africa*. Cape Town: Tafelberg.

Rupiah, M. 2005. 'Commentary. Zimbabwe: Governance through Military Operations', *African Security Review* 14(3): 6–10.

Said, E.W. 1978. *Orientalism*. New York: Vintage Books.

Sampson, A. 1999 (2000). *Mandela: The Authorised Biography*. London: HarperCollins.

Santos, B. de Sousa. 2007. 'Beyond Abyssal Thinking: From Global Lines to Ecologies of Knowledges', *Review* XXX(1): 45–89.

———. 2014. *Epistemologies of the South: Justice against Epistemicide*. Boulder, CO and London: Paradigm Publishers.

Schadeberg, J. (ed.). 1990. *Nelson Mandela and the Rise of the ANC*. Johannesburg: Jonathan Ball and Ad. Donker.

Schechter, D. 2013. *Madiba A to Z: The Many Faces of Nelson Mandela*. Johannesburg: Jacana Media.

Schreiner, O.C. 1923. *Thoughts on South Africa: Africana Reprint Library Volume Ten*. Johannesburg: Africana Book Society.

Schrire, R. 1991. *Adapt or Die: The End of White Politics in South Africa*. New York: Foreign Policy Association.

Seme, P.I. 1906. 'The Regeneration of Africa', in http://www.anc.org. za/show.php?id=4342 (accessed 28 March 2014).

Senghor, L. 1967. 'Socialism Is a Humanism', in E. Fromm (ed.), *Socialist Humanism: An International Symposium*. London: Allen Lane the Penguin Press, pp. 50–62.

Sitas, A. 2010. *The Mandela Decade 1990–2000: Labour, Culture and Society in Post-Apartheid South Africa*. Pretoria: UNISA Press.

Smith, A. (1776) 1976. *An Inquiry into the Nature and Causes of the Wealth of Nations*. Chicago: Chicago University Press.

Sonderling, S. 2012. 'Communication Is War By Other Means: A New Perspective on War and Communication in the Thought of Twentieth

Century Selected Communication Scholars'. Unpublished DLitt et Phil, University of South Africa.

South African Communist Party. 1985. *South African Communists Speak: Documents from the History of the South African Communist Party, 1915–1980*. London: Inkululeko Publishers.

Soyinka, W. 2006. 'Views from a Palette of the Cultural Rainbow', in X. Mangcu (ed.), *The Meaning of Mandela: A Literary and Intellectual Celebration*. Cape Town: HSRC Press, pp. 24–40.

———. 2012. *Of Africa*. New Haven, CT and London: Yale University Press.

Spivak, G.C. 1994. 'Can the Subaltern Speak?', in P. Williams and L. Chrisman (eds), *Colonial Discourses and Postcolonial Theory: A Reader*. New York: Columbia University Press, pp. 66–111.

Sriram, C.L. 2009. 'Introduction: Transitional Justice and Peacebuilding', in C.L. Sriram and S. Pillay (eds), *Peace versus Justice? The Dilemma of Transitional Justice in Africa*. Pietermaritzburg: University of KwaZulu-Natal Press, pp. 1–17.

Stengel, R. 2009. *Mandela's Way: Lessons on Life, Love and Courage*. New York: Crown.

Suttner, R. 2003. 'Early History of the African National Congress (ANC) Underground: From M-Plan to Rivonia', *South African Historical Journal* 49: 123–46.

———. 2007. '(Mis)Understanding Nelson Mandela', *African Historical Review* 39(2): 107–30.

Terreblanche, S. 2012. *Lost in Transition: South Africa's Search for a New Future since 1986*. Johannesburg: KMM Review Publishing Company.

Thompson, L. 2001. *A History of South Africa*. New Haven, CT and London: Yale University Press.

Tlostanova, M.V., and W.D. Mignolo. 2012. *Learning to Unlearn: Decolonial Reflections from Eurasia and the Americas*. Columbus: Ohio State University Press.

Verwoerd, W. 1997. 'Justice After Apartheid: Reflections on the South African Truth and Reconciliation Commission'. Unpublished paper presented at the 5th International Conference on Ethics and Development, Madras, India, 2–9 January.

Waldmeir, P. 1997. *Anatomy of a Miracle: The End of Apartheid and the Birth of a New South Africa*. New York: W.W. Norton.

Waters, M.-A. 1991. *Nelson Mandela and Fidel Castro: How Far We Slaves Have Come! South Africa and Cuba in Today's World*. New York and London: Pathfinder Press.

West, C. 1999. *The Cornell West Reader*. New York: Basic Books.

———. 2006. 'Nelson Mandela: Great Exemplar of the Grand Democratic Tradition', in X. Mangcu (ed.), *The Meaning of Mandela: A Literary and Intellectual Celebration*. Cape Town: HSRC Press, p. 23.

Wilderson, F.B. 2010. 'Obama and Mandela: The Parallels and the Differences'. Unpublished paper presented at the Concerned Citizens of Laguna Woods Village, 2 February.

*You Magazine: Special Issue on Mandela: Man of History*, April 2014.

Zeleza, P.T. 1997. *Manufacturing African Studies and Crises*. Dakar: CODESRIA Books.

———. 2003. *Rethinking Africa's Globalization, Volume 1: The Intellectual Challenges*. Trenton: Africa World Press.

———. 2013. 'Mandela's Long Walk with African History', *CODESRIA Bulletin* 3/4: 10–13.

Zizek, S. 2013. 'Mandela's Socialist Failure'. *New York Times*, 6 December.

# Index

Abacha, Sani 140–141
Academic-Institutional-Media 119
Achebe, Chinua 48, 129
Adebajo, Adekeye 3
African National Congress (ANC)
    xii, xiii, 9, 21, 23, 24, 28–37, 50,
    53–55, 56, 60, 71, 75, 78–82,
    85–90, 93, 95–103, 105, 106,
    108, 109, 111, 113, 114, 117,
    119, 120, 123, 141
African National Congress Youth
    League (ANCYL) 19, 79, 85
African nationalism 25, 68, 74–78,
    85
African nationalist historiography 7
African nationalist struggles xiii,
    26, 88
Afrikaner Weerstandsbeweging 102
Algerian National Liberation Front
    (FLN) 61
alterity 10, 124–126, 132, 135, 142
Amin, Samir 40
ANC see African National Congress
ANCYL (African National
    Congress Youth League) 19, 79,
    85
anti-apartheid
    campaign 139
    forces 98

resistance 87
    struggle 2, 50, 60, 86, 109
anti-colonial
    struggle see decolonial struggle
    violence 60, 61
antinomies (in Mandela's life) x, 9,
    12, 29, 72, 73–76
apartheid x, xi, xvi, xvii, 2–6, 9,
    12, 13, 16, 18, 23, 25–31, 36, 37,
    41, 42, 46, 48, 51, 56, 58–60, 68,
    74–76, 81, 86, 88, 90–92, 95–99,
    105, 106, 108–116, 118, 122,
    124, 125, 133, 136
    administrative 110, 113, 140
    architects 91
    colonialism xvi, 16, 25, 51, 77,
    90, 107, 113
    conflict 137, 138
    debt 115
    dismantled 106
    government 76, 81, 86, 89, 97,
    100, 101
    juridical xv, 109
    police 100
    regime 16, 87, 89, 90, 93–95, 97,
    100, 102, 104, 106, 108, 112, 117
APLA (Azanian People's Liberation
    Army) 114
Asmal, Kader 105

Athens-to-Washington paradigm 2, 38
Autshumayo 7, 62
Azania People's Organization (AZAPO) 102, 111
Azanian People's Liberation Army (APLA) 114
AZAPO (Azania People's Organization) 102, 111

Bantustans (Homelands) xvi, 115, 119
Barber, James 139, 140, 141
Barnard, Rita x, 29
Beresford, Alexander 58
Bhabha, Homi 49
Biko, Stephen Bantu xi, 136
Bill of Rights 52, 96
Black Consciousness Movement 14
blackism 10, 14, 127–129, 134
Blaut, James M xv, 39
Boehmer, Elleke xi
Boipatong Massacre 102
Bonner, Philip 74, 75
Botha, PW 75, 81, 91, 97, 116
Bulger, Patrick 73
Buthelezi, Gatsha Mangosuthu 101

Campbell, John 34
Campbell, Kermit E 116, 117
Carlin, John 116
Cartesian notion 44
Cartesian Subject(s) 45, 129–130, 132
CDE (critical decolonial ethics) xvi, 9, 10, 16, 27, 46, 48–50, 59, 76, 122
Cesaire, Aime 12, 46, 47, 136
Chabal, Patrick 133
Chinweizu 39, 50, 125
CODESA (Convention for a Democratic South Africa) 10, 24, 30, 54, 81, 82, 91–120, 137

Cold War xvii, 31, 51, 91, 93, 96, 97, 105, 107, 123, 137
colonialism x, xi, xiv, xv, 2, 4–6, 9, 13, 16, 25, 41, 42, 46–49, 51, 65, 66, 68–70, 75, 77, 90, 105, 107, 111, 113, 122, 126, 131, 133, 135–136
coloniality xiv-xviii, 1, 2, 16, 23, 29, 32, 35, 38, 44, 49–50, 61, 64, 66, 69–70, 122, 126, 132, 134, 135
Columbus, Christopher xvii, xviii, 45, 127, 134
Communist Party of South Africa (CPSA) 4, 96
Comprehensive Anti-Apartheid Act 97, 98
Congress of South African Trade Unions (COSATU) 98, 118
Congress of the People (COPE) 28
Conservative Party (CP) 102
Convention for a Democratic South Africa (CODESA) 10, 24, 30, 54, 81, 82, 91–120, 137
COPE (Congress of the People) 28
COSATU (Congress of South African Trade Unions) 98, 118
CP (Conservative Party) 102
CPSA (Communist Party of South Africa) 4, 96
critical decolonial ethics (CDE) xvi, 9, 10, 16, 27, 46, 48–50, 59, 76, 122
Cugoano, Ottobah 46

DA (Democratic Alliance) 3, 28
Da Gama, Vasco xvi, 127
Dalindyebo, Chief Jongintaba (David) 5, 17, 78, 83
Dalindyebo, Chief Meligqili 17, 18
Darwin, Charles 41
DBSA (Development Bank of South Africa) 99, 100

De Klerk, FW 2, 75, 81, 82, 91, 97, 100, 101, 103, 109
decolonial
ethics see critical decolonial ethics
humanism xii, xiii, xviii, 1–34, 36, 43, 46, 55, 91, 113–114, 122, 136, 138
humanist revolution ix, 8, 13, 115, 125
struggle xi, xii, 3, 5–9, 12, 14, 26, 36, 37, 57, 62, 70, 75–76, 120, 141
theory of life 35–70
'turn' 24, 48
decoloniality 9, 37, 40, 48–50, 67, 124
decolonization x, xii, xvii, xviii, 3, 4, 13, 15–16, 20, 26–27, 47, 51, 65–66, 70, 77–78, 123, 130, 134, 138, 140
Defiance Campaign 86
deimperialization xi, xii, xvii, xviii, 3, 4, 13, 15, 27, 47, 49, 70, 130, 134, 138, 140
Democratic Alliance (DA) 3, 28
deracialization xi, xviii, 115
Derrida, Jacques 49
Development Bank of South Africa (DBSA) 99, 100
Diaz, Bartholomew xvi
Die Stem 117
Du Bois, William EB xi, 12, 46, 48, 130, 132, 136
Du Preez Bezdrop, Anne Marie 75
Dube, Langalibalele 6, 36, 96
Dussel, Enrique xi, xii, 25, 38–40, 46

Economic Freedom Fighters (EFF) 29
Economic Trends Group (ETG) 118

EFF (Economic Freedom Fighters) 29
egocentrism 10, 37, 124–125
Ellis, Stephen 53, 54, 55
Eminent Persons Group (EPG) 97
empty lands xv, 125
Enlightenment xi, 10, 13–14, 44, 133
enslavement x, xvi, 6, 15, 24, 44, 125, 128, 133
EPG (Eminent Persons Group) 97
Escobar, Arturo 134
ETG (Economic Trends Group) 118
Euro-North America-centric modernity x-xii, 3, 17, 25, 32, 38, 40, 42, 44–46, 49, 51, 68, 122, 125, 127, 128, 131–132
Eurocentrism 2, 4, 9, 37–40, 48, 124, 128
Eze, Emmanuel Chukwudi 26

Fanon, Frantz xi, xii, xiv, 8, 12, 15, 46, 61–62, 68, 126, 136, 142
Fast Track Land Reform Programme 65, 67
female domesticity 75
Fifth Brigade atrocities 64
first humanist revolution 14
FLN (Algerian National Liberation Front) 61
foreign policy 138–142
Foucault, Michel 49
Freedom Charter 30, 36, 80, 121, 123

Gandhi, Mahatma xi, 46, 59, 62, 86, 123
Gandhism/Gandhianism 33, 59, 61, 86
Garveyism 13, 14
GEAR (Growth, Employment and Redistribution) 119, 120

Global North 49
Global South xvi, 10, 12, 15, 37,
    42, 46, 49, 124, 134, 142
Goldberg, Dennis 80
Goody, Jack 2, 39
Gorbachev, Michael 97
Gordon, Lewis R 115, 127, 129,
    131
Graaff, Sir De Villiers 94
Gramsci, Antonio 49
Groote Schuur Minute 100
Grosfoguel, Ramon xi, 41, 44–45,
    49, 70, 129, 135
Growth, Employment and
    Redistribution (GEAR) 119, 120

Habib, Adam 107, 108, 140
Halisi, CRD 28, 55, 56, 57
Hani, Chris 82, 102, 109
Harare Declaration 81, 101
Hellenocentrism 9, 37–40, 128
Heraclitus 41
Hobbes, Thomas 41
Homelands (Bantustans) xvi, 115,
    119
Hyslop, Jonathan 61, 62

Ibekwe, Chinweizu 39, 50, 125
ICC (International Criminal Court)
    2, 137
IDRC (International Development
    Research Centre) 118
IFP (Inkatha Freedom Party) 81,
    101
IMF (International Monetary Fund)
    120
imperialism x, xi, xv, 2, 4, 6, 9, 15,
    25, 41–42, 46, 48–49, 52, 68,
    122, 126, 133, 136
Inkatha Freedom Party (IFP) 81,
    101
International Criminal Court (ICC)
    2, 137

International Development
    Research Centre (IDRC) 118
International Monetary Fund (IMF)
    120

James, CLR x-xi, 46, 134, 136

Kant, Immanuel 14
Kathrada, Ahmed 81, 108, 109
Kaunda, Kenneth 46–47
Kenyatta, Jomo 63, 88
Khoi 24
Khoi Khoi 7
Khoisan 7
King, Martin Luther 59, 123
King Shaka 62
Kotane, Moses 20, 33, 55

Lancaster House negotiations 64
Le Pere, Garth 53, 54
Lembede, Anton Muzwake 19, 20,
    79, 85
Leninism 85
liberalism 33, 49, 55, 57, 62
liberation struggle x, 5, 9, 13,
    32–33, 54–57, 59, 63, 66, 75–76,
    84, 86, 88, 90–91, 93, 106, 108,
    124, 141
Lodge, Tom 53, 72, 73
Luthuli, Chief Albert xiii, 23, 36,
    46, 85, 87

Macro-Economic Research Group
    (MERG) 118
Magubane, Bernard Makhosezwe 6
Maharaj, Mac 80
Maldonado-Torres, Nelson xv, 10,
    13, 24, 44–46, 48, 62, 115, 125,
    132
Malema, Julius 29
Mamdani, Mahmood xiii, xiv, xviii,
    77, 84, 104–108, 110–111, 114,
    136–137

Mandela, Nomzamo Winfred (Winnie) Madikizela 74–75, 80, 82, 84
Mandela, Nosekeni 80
Mandela phenomenon x, xi, xiii, 1–34, 37, 53–59, 62, 120, 122, 127, 135, 142
Mandela Rhodes Foundation 2
Mandela's life history 78–83
Mangcu, Xolela xviii
Marx, Karl 127, 128
Marxism 20, 49, 55–57, 85
Mase, Evelyn 79, 80, 84
Maylam, Paul 3, 32, 34,
Mbeki, Thabo 23–24, 54, 89, 137, 141
Mbembe, Achille 27, 49, 61
Mda, Peter 79
Mda, Zakes 31
MEC (Mineral Energy Complex) 98–100
Mendieta, Eduardo 46
MERG (Macro-Economic Research Group) 118
Mhlaba, Raymond 81
Mineral Energy Complex (MEC) 98–100
MK (uMkonto we Sizwe) 59, 72, 82, 86, 89, 102
Mkandawire, Thandika 122
Mkhonto we Sizwe see uMkonto we Sizwe
Mkonto we Sizwe see uMkonto we Sizwe
Mlangeni, Andrew 81
Mngxitama, Andile 30
Mphakanyiswa, Gadla Henry 78
MPNF (Multiparty Negotiating Forum) 102
Mqhayi, Krune 18, 19
Mqhekezweni 78, 83
Mudimbe, Valentin Y 132
Mugabe, Robert Gabriel 51, 63–68, 88

Multiparty Negotiating Forum (MPNF) 102
Mulugushi Declaration 47
Munro, Brenna 75
Muzondidya, James 67
Mveso 78, 83

nation building 10, 77, 113–118
National Party (NP) 98–100
Ndebele-speaking people 64, 65
Ndlovu, Sifiso Mxolisi 89–90, 93–95, 120
negritude 13, 14, 47, 48, 127
NEM (Normative Economic Model 99
neo-colonialism xv, 25, 42, 122, 133
neo-liberalism 3, 9, 31, 93, 98–99, 119
Netshitenzhe, Joel 113
Ngwane, Zolani 74
Nietzsche, Friedrich xiii, 15, 41
Nkomo, Joshua 64, 88
Nkomo, William 20, 79
Nkrumah, Kwame 47, 88, 123
non-violence 60, 86
Normative Economic Model (NEM) 99
NP (National Party) 98–100
Nuremberg xiii, xvii, 2, 10, 91, 104, 106–107, 110, 122, 137
Nuttall, Sarah 27
Nyerere, Julius 47, 51, 63, 77, 136

ontological density x, 15, 24, 47–48, 51, 69, 114, 132, 135
Oppenheimer, Harry 99

PAC (Pan-Africanist Congress) 81, 102, 114
PAFMECSA (Pan-African Freedom Movement for East, Central and Southern Africa) 80

Pan-African Freedom Movement
for East, Central and Southern
Africa (PAFMECSA) 80
pan-African integration 77
Pan-Africanism 13, 14, 47, 57,
127, 134
Pan-Africanist Congress (PAC) 81,
102, 114
paradigm of peace xi, xiii, xvi, 2, 7,
9–10, 12–13, 16, 26–27, 37, 42,
44–48, 50–52, 101, 104, 121–142
paradigm of war xi, xii, xiv, xvi,
xv, 1, 2, 6, 8, 9, 10–12, 15, 16,
26, 27, 35, 37, 41, 42, 44 48, 50,
65, 66, 100–101, 104, 122, 124,
36, 139–140, 142
Patriotic Front 64
Peet, Richard 119
Pillay, Suren 103, 104
pluriversal
humanism xvi, 2, 7, 12, 16, 26,
120, 124
humanity 49
political community 109
society xvii, 13, 114, 115
world xviii, 10, 16, 24, 136, 140
pluriversalism 9, 27
pluriversality xi, 15, 50, 142
political consciousness (Mandela's)
83, 84–91
Pollsmoor Prison 80, 81, 88
post-apartheid
government 98
nation 56
society 36, 104, 110–111, 114,
119
South Africa ix, 31, 99, 113,
115, 117 139
state 56
postcolonialism 49–50
postmodernism 49
poststructuralism 49
Pretoria Minute 101

Quijano, Anibal 16, 38
Qunu 78, 83

Radebe, Gaur 19, 79
Ramphela, Mamphela 105, 110,
112
RDP (Reconstruction and
Development Programme)
118–119
Reagan, Ronald 97
Reconstruction and Development
Programme (RDP) 118–119
Record of Understanding 102
Renaissance 10, 13–14, 44
restorative justice 136–138
Reykjavik Summit 97
Rhodes, Cecil John 2, 3
Rhodes Must Fall Movement 3
Rhodes' statue 3
Rhodes Trust 3
Rivonia Trials 34, 55, 59, 74, 80,
87, 116
Robben Island xvii, 7, 55, 80,
87–88, 91, 116
Rupiya, Martin 65

SACP see South African
Communist Party
SADET (South African Democracy
and Education Trust) 93
SADF (South African Defence
Force) 111, 114
Said, Edward W 39, 49
Sampson, Anthony 25, 88
San 7, 24
SANDF (South African National
Defence Force) 114
Sankara, Thomas xi, 46, 123, 136
SANNC (South African National
Native Congress) 93
Santos, Boaventura de Sousa xvii,
131
SAP (South African Police) 111

SAP (Structural Adjustment
  Programme) 119
SAPS (South African Police
  Service) 115
Saro-Wiwa, Ken 140
Sartre, Jean-Paul 15
Schechter, Danny 76, 90
Schreiner, Olive Cronwright 21, 22
Schrire, Robert 100
Sebokeng massacre 100
second humanist revolution 14
Seme, Pixley ka Isaka xiii, 23, 36,
  96
Senghor, Leopold Sedar 47
Shaka, King 62
Sisulu, Walter 33, 79, 81, 85
Sitas, Ari 109
slave trade x, xiv, 6, 25, 41–42, 46,
  48–49, 68, 69, 122, 133, 136
slavery xiv, 14, 41
Slovo, Joe 4, 53, 101, 103, 105
Smith, Adam 127
Sobukwe, Robert Mangaliso 19, 20
South Africa Chamber of Business
  99
South African Communist Party
  (SACP) 4, 20–21, 29, 53, 54–56,
  81, 96, 101–102
South African Defence Force
  (SADF) 111, 114
South African Democracy and
  Education Trust (SADET) 93
South African National Defence
  Force (SANDF) 114
South African National Native
  Congress (SANNC) 93
South African nationalism 55
South African Police (SAP) 111
South African Police Service
  (SAPS) 115
Soyinka, Wole 35, 126
Spivak, Gayatri 49
Sriram, Chandra Lekha 103

Stengel, Richard 58
Structural Adjustment Programme
  (SAP) 119
Stuurman, Klaas 7
survivor's justice xiii, xiv, 1, 2,
  107–108
Suttner, Raymond 32–34, 53, 59,
  60

Tambo, Oliver R 79, 82, 87, 89
TerreBlanche, Eugene 116
Terreblanche, Sampie 96, 98–100
Thatcher, Margaret 97
Thembu
  background 4
  family 71
  people 83
Thiong'o, Ngugi wa xi, 48,
  126–127
Third Chimurenga 65
Third Humanist Revolution 6, 8,
  13–17, 42–44, 46, 124
Thompson, Leonard 90, 102, 112,
  114
TRC (Truth and Reconciliation
  Commission) 83, 109–114, 115,
  116
Truth and Reconciliation
  Commission (TRC) 83, 109–
  114, 115, 116
Tutu, Archbishop Desmond 88,
  112, 118

Ubuntu 5, 23, 47, 50, 136
uMkonto we Sizwe (MK) 59, 72,
  82, 86, 89, 102
United States Congress 52, 59, 79,
  97–98
United States of America 2, 39,
  96–98, 141
Unity Accord 64
University of Fort Hare 79, 84

Verwoerd, Hendrik Frensch 94, 116
Victor Verster Prison 81, 88
victor's justice xiii, 105, 107–108

Wa Thiong'o, Ngugi xi, 48, 126–127
Washington Consensus 9, 99
West, Cornell ix, 129
Westernization 9, 37–40, 128
Wilderson, Frank B 106, 123
will to live xii, 5, 8, 25, 35, 40–42, 61
will to power xii, xiii, 8, 15, 25, 32, 35, 40–42
Willemse, Genl Johan 116
World Bank 120
World Trade Centre 82, 102

xenophobia 16, 65, 68, 125–126, 139
Xhosa
  people/nation/tribe 18
  governance 78
  identity 83
  tradition/custom 74, 83
Xuma, Dr Alfred Bitini 79

Yutar, Percy 116

Zeleza, Paul Tiyambe 2, 38, 76, 77, 123
Zille, Helen 3
Zizek, Slavoj 26, 51, 73
Zuma, President Jacob 55

www.ingramcontent.com/pod-product-compliance
Lightning Source LLC
Chambersburg PA
CBHW060041030426
42334CB00019B/2426